Chase the Wonder

Stories of Christmas to Fill our Hearts with Hope

Matt Manney

Dedication:

To the child once filled with wonder in all of us ...

—Give the grown-up version of you a little time,
and we'll be reunited again.

The world will be a better place for it.

Table of Contents

Introduction

Chasing Christmas

Christmas today is a far cry from the very first Christmas so many years ago. The crazy, frenzied chaos of the season can overwhelm us. The stress, pressure, and tension can make us resent what should be the most wonderful time of the year. For some, it may be the first Christmas without the one you lost, who you loved so very much. Christmas just isn't the same anymore.

Over the years, I've watched my soul ebb and flow with the wonder of Christmas. I've had to stop myself on more than one Christmas Eve and do a mental slap in the face to check my attitude at the moment.

This book is a call to regain what we tend to lose with time as life goes on. The most incredible gift, the most historic moment and dramatic event took place over two thousand years ago, and we use the holiday of Christmas to celebrate that moment. Sometimes, though, the manger can become crowded with Santa, car commercials with a big red bow, and eggnog frappuccinos.

In this book, I share stories that I hope will take you back in time to your childhood, your first loves, and your most precious memories to help you recapture what may have been lost with time. Even if you have a difficult past, I believe there are memories and moments that you can redeem. My goal is to help us hear the message God spoke to each of the characters who had a stake in the unfolding Christmas story. The messages God spoke to Mary, Joseph, the shepherds, wise men, and even King Herod are messages He still speaks to us today. I want to help you renew your view and vision of your past to help you have a sense of joy and wonder for the future.

Wonder is a word that has worked its way into the Christmas narrative. Wonder, in and of itself, can be a little tough to describe. For me, wonder is the joy, anticipation, curiosity, and hope of good to come.

God uses the wonder of Christmas to draw each one of us into the story, to find the part we play in the manger scene. Whatever message we need from God, He speaks it to us through his story of the manger. As you read the story of Christmas as it unfolds in these pages, it may be the first time or the thousandth time you've heard the story. My hope for you is that the story rekindles your love for life, for God, for the loved ones around you, and for the wonder of Jesus. The wonder of Christmas will pull you into this grand and glorious adventure of life. If you've lost the wonder, may you recapture Christmas for all its joy, happiness, and splendor as God intended so long ago when the angels sang "Glory to God in the highest, peace on earth, good will toward men."

Wonder is the ability to smile, laugh, and love just as the shepherds and wise men did so long ago after their encounter with the one we celebrate each 25th of December: Jesus, the Christ of Christmas. Join me as we chase the wonder of our Savior Jesus and his story from long ago.

Chapter One

Delight of Anticipation

I closed my eyes as tight as I could. I didn't want to see a thing. I didn't want to ruin anything. It's the number one rule every excited child understands on Christmas Eve: Santa knows when you are sleeping; he knows when you're awake. I felt the cool, smooth sheets against my skin. My toes wiggled with restless delight. It was only one more sleep until Christmas.

Just a few hours before, my family and I sat in the church across the cornfield behind our house. The candlelight service was filled with Christmas carols and special songs prepared by the children's choir and other selected vocalists. My brother and I sat still in our best church clothes while we listened to the pastor give a few thoughts about the Christmas story. At one point, an older man in the church invited all the kids to the front to sit and listen to the traditional Christmas story. I was too shy to go upfront and too occupied with my thoughts about what would take place later that night.

As traditions go, we would come home after the service, change into our pajamas, and wait for my dad to pick out a small gift to give each of us on Christmas Eve. It was just a teaser of things to come. Then it was time to do one last thing before going to bed: prepare Santa's midnight snack.

I set out a small salad plate with three chocolate chip cookies—one for Santa to eat right away, one for the trip back up the chimney, and one for the road. Standing like a tin soldier next to the plate was a tall glass of cold milk. I laid out a few gnarled carrots for the reindeer for good measure. Then it was time for bed.

My mom pulled the Mickey Mouse comforter close around my neck and shoulders. I had been a little obsessive-compulsive about being tucked in ever since my brother told me a ghost story he'd heard at camp the previous summer about a headless man who roamed the camp looking for unsuspecting junior campers not tucked in their bunk. I wasn't about to forfeit my head on the most magical night of the whole year! Looking back, I realize the camp counselors told that story to keep kids in their bunks. But the story for this night was about good ol' St. Nick. There was no need to threaten us with ghost stories—just a lump of coal or Santa passing over the house completely would do.

I lay in bed with my eyes closed and my mind wide open in wonder. What would the morning hold?

The following morning, I woke to the sun sneaking past drawn drapes in my darkened bedroom. I pulled back my Mickey Mouse comforter, slipped into my slippers, and dashed into the hall and down the stairs. As I approached the last step, I turned just to my left and peered around the wall leading to the living room. My final image of this room the previous night had been that of a dark space lit only by the twinkling white lights of the Christmas tree, a plate of cookies, and empty space beneath the Christmas tree.

In my mind, I was hoping the plate would be picked clean, the glass empty, and the carrots gone. Why? Because that would mean Santa had come and presents would be his trade-off for the midnight snack. I had been so good all year long—or at least that's what I hoped Santa would say.

I looked for the little plate on the side table I had left the night before. Sure enough, the plate and cup were both empty, and next to the plate lay a picture. I walked over and picked it up. It was a Polaroid of the back of Santa Claus, standing in our living room. I quickly looked up and spied the tree. I saw the star at the top, the homemade ornaments, and lights strung in a zig-zag swag back and forth on the tree. Candy canes hung from the ends of the pine branches. I finally looked to the bottom of the tree ... piles of presents. Each pile was distinctively wrapped. Some had bright, colorful paper, some had cartoon characters, others were red with green flourishes, and some were white with happy snowmen on them. *Which pile is mine? I can't wait to find out which pile is mine.*

From the kitchen came smells of coffee brewing, cream-chipped beef cooking, and English muffins toasting. I could faintly hear Nat King Cole singing "Chestnuts roasting on an open fire..." followed by the clink of dishes and cooking utensils.

"Hey sweetheart," my mom called from the kitchen doorway. "How did you sleep last night?"

"I couldn't. I was too excited," I said.

"I'm sure you didn't," she said with a smile.

"Why don't you grab your stocking and have a seat on the couch. Mike is helping your dad in the kitchen. Dad will read the Christmas story, and you can open your stocking while you're listening," she said.

"Then we open presents?" I asked.

"Then we open presents," mom said.

———————

I wasn't a die-hard kid on the whole Santa deal. I don't know when I stopped believing. Maybe it was when I spied a bag of Christmas presents tucked away in the back of my parent's closet under an old flannel blanket. Or it could have been the fact that the Santa at the annual Rotary Club Christmas breakfast smelled more like beef and cheese than candy canes and fresh-baked sugar cookies. At some point, I stopped leaving the plate with cookies, stopped writing the letters and wish lists, and stopped believing.

Belief is a funny thing. It's more than an intellectual assent to a standard line of thinking. It is more than a set of facts, dogmas, and truths. Belief to a child is the anticipation of good that is to come. Belief could also be called hope. At some point, the anticipation comes face-to-face with life. Hopes don't happen. Dreams are disappointed. Beliefs transform to doubt. "Hope so" thinking turns to "don't know" disbelief. What's a person to do when they forfeit the most precious gift a child has ever been given: belief? What do you do when the anticipation and happiness fades? What can you do to regain the wonder and excitement of a child-like belief?

When beliefs flicker out, our faith must run deep.

Chapter Two

More than Meets the Eye

On another night two thousand years ago, another young believer was being tucked into bed. She lived in a humble stone and plaster home her father had built for her mother years ago. The dry, hot days gave way to cool, silent nights. She had gone through the customary training like so many other children her age. Raised in a devout Jewish home, her family attended worship at the synagogue each Sabbath and were sure to be in their place to observe the high holidays each year.

While her family was not rich, her father, Eli,[1] told her stories of the riches of the kings of old. As he tucked her in bed along with her sisters each night,[2] he would tell them stories of their people who walked the earth centuries before them.

He whispered in hushed tones, "And King Solomon's vast wealth of gold and silver was so plentiful it flowed through the streets. The blessing of God was upon his people. Solomon had a brother, Nathan, who is in our family tree. Their father was David, the greatest king our people have ever known and your great-great … (well, it's a lot of greats!) grandfather. Because of his love and adherence to God, God blessed him. While Grandpa David was not a perfect ruler, he was a man after God's own heart. Because of David's love and obedience to God, God told him he would give birth to a ruler greater than all the kings and queens our people would ever know, a king to rule with justice, peace, and love," he said with a twinkle in his eye.

"Papa, could I be a princess one day?" Mary asked. "Mary, if you follow God and love him with all your heart, God will do things in your life unlike any of our people have ever known. God has promised to visit his people again one day, and maybe—just maybe—you'll be there to see it. But for now, little one, you need to sleep. Jehovah won't be coming to bless any tired little girls unless you get to sleep," he said as he kissed her head.

Mary began her schooling at the local synagogue at age five. Along with the other boys and girls, she learned how to read and write and studied the history of the Hebrews. She would learn the commandments of Jehovah in terms of the laws of the Jews as outlined in the holiest writings of the Torah.[3] As she got older, she would learn more about the writings of the ancient prophets and the hope of deliverance to come one day through the rightful heir to the throne of King David. For now, she would wait and hope while the Roman oppression ruled with an iron fist.

As was customary, the boys and girls became legal adults at the age of thirteen. Boys who showed an aptitude for the law would continue their education at the synagogue. Boys who didn't pursue an education at the synagogue would go into a trade, most likely their father's. The girl's path was much different. At the age of thirteen, she would begin to prepare herself to be a wife. Most girls were betrothed to a boy three to five years older than they were. [4]

In Mary's case, she was engaged to be married to a man named Joseph. Their parents had arranged the marriage as was tradition, and the fathers settled on the appropriate price for the dowry. Mary and Joseph most likely knew each other while growing up together in their small town of Nazareth.

Arrangements would begin to take place. Mary would prepare for the wedding while Joseph built on to his father's house to prepare his own place to call home with Mary. He would have carefully chosen each basalt stone, "dressed" each stone to square it just right, and completed the addition with a mud plaster finish and a wooden front door. [5]

The young couple followed in the cultural tradition of their parents, grandparents, and so on. They had grown up in a home where faith and family were the focus. The traditions fostered a sense of hope, certainty, and simplicity that would be the foundation of the family they would raise one day. Mary was crossing the threshold into adulthood, a journey young Jewish girls would have dreamed of, just as little girls hold on to hopes and dreams today.

God was going to place Mary's plans on hold. He

was about to do something for which there was no precedent. A visitor was about to come to give a message Mary's people had waited four hundred years to hear: God was coming to be with his people once again.

Christmas with its bright lights, presents, Hallmark Channel specials, and holiday carols is a far cry from the lead-up to the very first Christmas, yet the spirit of anticipation has carried on. The crisis Mary was about to face is not too far from difficulties so many of us face today. There was no lesson at synagogue Mary could look to for instruction or guidance.

God does that sometimes in our lives, too. The exact circumstances of the challenges we face give us little to go on. We find, with time, our faith is tested and our hope placed on the chopping block of life experience. All we thought we knew to be true is put to the test. There is no final exam—oral, written or otherwise—given by the ruler of the synagogue. This was a life test for Mary, and those are the hardest ones. The outcomes for life tests have more at stake—more to lose and more to gain.

What I find so amazing as we jump into Mary's story is what the author doesn't tell us but is surely implied and understood. Mary is going to hear from an angel, and not just any angel: Gabriel. Gabriel is God's chief messenger angel. What we'll discover from Gabriel's declaration is that there is more to Mary than meets the eye. Mary is about to face a test that will cripple her belief in the God she learned about in synagogue, around the oven with her mother baking bread, and alongside her father patching the clay on the roof of their small home on the hillside of Nazareth. Mary is either going to lose sight of her belief or allow the circumstances to drive her faith deep.

Christmas is much more than meets the eye.

Chapter Three

Fierce Faithed Girl

The car horn beeped twice. "Matthew, it's time to go. Your ride is here," my mom called. I grabbed my California Raisins backpack, my brown paper bag lunch, and my Christmas money envelope. This is the day I had been looking forward to since my kindergarten teacher made the announcement just after we came back from Thanksgiving break. Our little, Second Avenue Elementary School, was hosting a Christmas shopping experience for each class. Vendors came to the gymnasium, set up their displays on six-foot-long wooden tables, and laid out an assortment of knick-knacks, tchotchkes, and trinkets that little kids love and parents put up with.

My ride had just pulled up. The little girl I carpooled with—a quiet girl with long dark hair and an olive complexion—lived at the other end of the neighborhood in a cul-de-sac. Her family's station wagon was our transportation to the school only a few miles away. I ran down the driveway, backpack bouncing up and down as I went. I pulled open the door handle and slid onto the tan, vinyl-upholstered bench next to her.

"Did you bring your money?" I asked. She nodded yes. That was the extent of our conversation for the ride that day.

We pulled up to the student drop-off area in front of the school and piled out of the wagon. Kids were everywhere, some filing out of bright yellow school buses and others bounding out of their parent's vehicles.

This was my first chance to do Christmas shopping for my family. The school sent home an information sheet explaining the Christmas shopping experience. Each child was to bring in just a few dollars to spend for the day. I had a five dollar bill in my little white envelope that was burning a hole in my pocket.

As soon as we got into the classroom, my teacher collected our money envelopes. "Matthew, can I have your envelope, please?" my teacher asked. I was a little hesitant. She reassured me this was standard procedure. "I trust you, Matthew. It's just a mandate handed down from years of experience," she explained.

"What's a mandrake?" I asked.

"Next, please," she called to my carpool buddy.

When the time finally came, we lined up at the door and prepared to descend on Santa's workshop in the gym. As we entered, teachers and parents were milling around helping kids with their selections and purchases. Five whole dollars. Look at all I could get with five whole dollars! The dilemma I soon found myself in was that my desire to give out-paced my capacity to give. I had just enough to get an oven mitt with holly berries and leaves on it and a set of matching white candles with little wax snowmen attached halfway up the stick. It turned out I just had enough money to get my mom's presents for Christmas. My dad and Mike … well, I guess they be good with a stick of gum. Not just any gum—Bubblicious Strawberry Banana flavored gum.

I can distinctly remember being torn inside because I couldn't make my money stretch.

I learned a lesson early in life: what we want to do

will often be in tension with what we can do.

———————

In the book of Luke, Doctor Luke writes to a friend by the name of Theophilus. Theo is Greek by ethnicity. From what we understand, he has a close relationship with Luke. Luke goes to great lengths to explain the whole story of Jesus to Theo in what has become known as Luke's Gospel. As any good doctor, Luke was keen on detail, directing our attention to the aspects of the story that help us understand the importance of a young Jewish girl being brought into the massive narrative God is unfolding.

Luke writes for Theo: "(Mary) was visited by the angel Gabriel ... and he said, 'Hail, thou that art highly favored, the Lord is with thee: blessed art thou among women.'"[1] I'm sure the old English was a little much for her to process. Just kidding. (Most likely, the greeting would have been in first-century Greek, possibly even in Hebrew or Aramaic.)

She was puzzled by the angel's greeting.

First, no one had heard from God or had a vision,

let alone seen an angel, in four hundred years. For all the Jews knew, God had abandoned them. It's easy to question your relationships when you've been ghosted. Second, she was a teenager. How was she so favored above all women? How did the angel know her reputation? Had he been spying on her? She knew angels were powerful, but they weren't God. So, what was the deal? Third and finally, what did he mean by "God is with you?" Again, God hadn't been present and revealing Himself in hundreds of years. Why would he pick a teenager, of all people, to receive a message from God? What about the ruler of the synagogue, the Pharisees, or even the Sadducees? Wouldn't they be the ones to welcome such a venerable guest into their home and handle such a profound announcement?

Gabriel tells Mary, "God has chosen you to have a son, and he's even picked out a name: Jesus."

"Wait, what?" she responds. "How is this possible since I haven't been with a man?"

"It's going to be a miracle. God is going to place within you His very own son," Gabe explains. "As a confirmation, God has allowed your cousin Elizabeth to become pregnant in her old age. She's six months along. She was unable to have any children and now look at her," he says. "When God wants to move and make things happen, there is nothing impossible for Him to do."

Mary's response is, "I'm on board. Just what you've said, let it happen to me."[2] With that, Gabriel disappears.

Can you imagine? In a moment, her plans to get married to the love of her life, Joseph, would be placed on hold.

Think about it. Imagine the range of emotions she must have felt: "How incredible! I'm going to have a baby. I wonder what he'll look like. And was that truly an angel that just spoke to me? God's promise is going to be fulfilled to Grandpa David, and I'm a part of the plan. But what about Joseph? What will Joseph say? What will he think? Will he believe me when he finds out I'm pregnant? Will he still marry me? Will he still trust me? Will he still love me? I was planning a wedding shower. Now I'm planning a baby shower. What will people think?"

What do you do when God changes your plans? What happens when what God has called you to do conflicts with what you desire to do? That goes against our wiring. If I do what God says, if I obey, if I love God, He is guaranteed to bless me. In our Western, Christmas, commercial, and consumer mindset we fall prey to the thinking that God will do our will for us if we comply with what we think He wants from us.

How do you reconcile the Christmas story? God sets the stage for one of the biggest scandals the little town of Nazareth has ever seen. The grand entrance of His only begotten Son would be shrouded under a haze of scandal. Mary would learn a profound lesson I believe she learned at a young age: even when life is not working around you, God is at work in you.

Chapter Four

Waiting in Wonder

The car door shut with force. Silence. "Mom, I just don't get why you won't let me," I said. Being a nine-year-old a few months before Christmas and begging for toys doesn't make for a very good combination.

The housing development we lived in at the time was just a five-minute drive from a Jamesway. Think of it as a K-Mart or Walmart. As a kid, I went through several intense obsessive toy phases.

There was the die-cast plane phase. Any money I received for my birthday, special occasion, or otherwise was invested in matchbox-size planes. Speaking of matchboxes, I went through a phase of collecting small cars, called Micro Machines, and other vehicles. My LEGO® phase was an expensive one.

Basketball cards were a hefty hobby, as well. A sports card shop just happened to be a few blocks from my dad's auto repair shop, where my brother, sister, and I spent a lot of time while my mom picked up car parts for my dad or ran errands. I would try to find some excuse to steal away to the sports card shop. The owner, Mr. Rivera, was a nice guy. He was a pastor and ran the sports card shop on the side. I went to school with his two boys. I'd ride my bike the few blocks to the card shop and buy the latest Michael Jordan card he had in the display case. Most often, I'd wind up trying to negotiate the price on an entire box of cards still in the factory wrapper. I'd carefully unwrap the cellophane from the box, pull back the cardboard tabs, and open the box to reveal dozens and dozens of unopened packs of basketball cards. I would meticulously go through each pack and start putting the cards in order by the number on the back of the card. If I was lucky, I'd find a complete set as I unwrapped each pack. If I was missing any cards from the set, I wouldn't rest until I had a complete set for my collection.

G.I. Joes, small cardboard discs called POGS, Teenage Mutant Ninja Turtles action figures, Nintendo video games—on the list went. Like any kid, I enjoyed toys, but my problem was the timing. I didn't like to wait; I wanted the toy now. My attitude was a little reminiscent of Veruca Salt from Willy Wonka and the Chocolate Factory: "I want it now!" It wasn't that bad, but you get the idea.

"Sweetheart, I can't keep letting you get G.I. Joes," my mom said. "But why?" I asked. "Because Christmas is only a few months away and I don't have the money to spend on anything extra right now," she said. How many of us have said that to our kids? I didn't understand then, but now that I'm a dad to four, I find myself doing a lot of explaining to my toy-negotiating connoisseurs. What I know now is the importance of anticipation, delayed gratification, and patience.

The closer we would get to Christmas, the harder the pressure I'd put on my parents. The window shopping, television commercials, and kids at school who would bring in their latest toy didn't help. You know—the kids who didn't have parents like yours or mine. They had extremely kind parents who complied with their every whim, request, and fancy. They had parents who loved them and adored them, unlike yours or mine. I'm exaggerating, of course, but just seeing them with their new toys a few weeks before Christmas was a tough pill to swallow!

Waiting is not a naturally intrinsic human quality. Some people have the patience of Job, but most of us don't. I know, I know—you're like Job and have lots of patience and can't understand why the rest of the schleps in the world can't wait. But I'd imagine waiting in line at the grocery store or sitting in your car, stuck behind the guy on his phone not paying attention to a green light, would bring a little impatience out of you.

Do you remember the feeling, though? The tension of wanting something. You know—the feeling of anticipation, waiting for Christmas morning to come and desperately hoping the very thing you longed for was neatly wrapped in a pretty box with a bow and tucked safely under your Christmas tree. That longing translates to so many other areas of life. We wait for graduation day to come—kindergarten graduation, that is. Then to get into the double birthday digits, to become an official teenager, to graduate from middle school, high school, and maybe college. Then it's the life stage of waiting: waiting to find out if you got the job—your first job, that is. You went through a season of waiting to get married, to have your first kid, your first home, your next kid, maybe your second marriage, for the kids to leave home, then the grandkids. What do you have left to look forward to? Your funeral, I guess.

Mary faced waiting, just like you and me—nine months, to be exact.

————

I would love to know what the conversations were like in Mary's home. What did she say to her parents? How did her siblings take it? What did her in-laws think? We get a glimpse into Joseph's thoughts, but what did the conversations sound like?

Mary's mother and father had their own set of feelings, hopes, and dreams about their daughter. They had a reputation to uphold, friends to give explanations to, and the fear of losing their place at the local synagogue. If word got out about Mary's unexpected pregnancy, what would they tell people? Would people believe Mary's story, that an angel spoke to her? No one had heard from God, let alone an angel, in centuries. What was so special about Mary that she heard from God via an angel? How would they explain that the pregnancy wasn't just any baby but the Messiah, the promised Son of God? Can you see how difficult it must have been for them to process?

"Mary, what do you mean you saw an angel last night?" her mother asked.

"I mean that on my way back from the well, I was just pouring water into one of our pots next to the house, and I sensed this bright light from behind me," Mary explained. "When I turned around, the angel Gabriel was standing before me. I didn't know what to do except shield my eyes from the bright light. The intensity of the light diminished, and then he told me what I just told you: I am going to become pregnant. It is a miraculous act of God."

"Mary, please don't be blasphemous. You know what kind of trouble this could get you into. Don't even tease about such a thing," her mother said.

"Mother, I know what you are saying, but please

hear me. You know me. You know how much I love Joseph. I would never betray his trust. I don't know why God chose me. I don't know why now, just before I am to be married to Joseph, this would happen. But what I do know is that God is working in me something I could only dream of."

"But Mary, how do you know this thing is of God?"

"Mother, Gabriel told me our cousin Elizabeth is expecting, as well," Mary said.

"Oh, Mary, Elizabeth is far too old to have a child! She has been barren her whole life."

"No, Mother, it's true. Find out for yourself. She is six months along. Surely you will see with your own eyes the work of God! I can't explain it. I don't understand it, but God is doing something. It is a wonder. All I can do now is to wait and prepare for this baby, my baby to come," Mary said.

―――――――

Anticipation does something within us. It creates wonder and excitement for some. For others, regardless of how good the thing to come may be, they worry while they wait.

We glamorize Mary and her being "with child." We strip from the story the humanity and difficulty she faced. We look at Mary as the "golden ticket" winner. In the bigger picture, she truly was favored, yet she would also taste the most soul-crushing agony any mother could ever experience in witnessing the death of her son only three decades later.

For now, the excitement carried her from Nazareth to visit her cousin Elizabeth in the city of Juda. The thing God was doing was about to be confirmed by his miraculous working in Elizabeth. Mary wasn't crazy, lying, or looking for attention. God's confirmation would help her anticipate all he was about to work in and through her life.

Chapter Five

Preparing for Joy

Christmas of 1988 was one of my first memorable Christmases. While preparing for the holidays, my mom was pregnant with my sister Sarah. Since going through four pregnancies with my wife Amanda, I've learned that the process of pregnancy has good parts and not-so-pleasant parts (not that I was the one to carry the kids in my stomach for nine months). The morning sickness, cravings, doctor visits, making sure the baby is okay and healthy, preparing to bring this little life into a great big world—those are no easy tasks. Then there's baby-proofing the house, working out schedules, setting up the nursery, preparing for family to come and help, and receiving well wishes from friends and colleagues. Amanda was only pregnant with one of our kids during the holidays—Maggie. She was almost eight months pregnant with Maggie when we celebrated Christmas.

For my mom to have my sister December 30th, the week between Christmas and New Year's, must have been exciting and stressful. As a six-year-old, I'll never forget. It was a Friday, and my dad had picked my brother Mike and me up from my grandparents. He had been at the hospital with my mom and planned to come get us once Sarah was born. We drove to the hospital, and I kept wondering what she would look like and sound like. Would she be like a Cabbage Patch doll with cute curly hair? Or would she look all wrinkly like a troll with the neon pink crazy hair? I'd seen babies before, but when it's a sibling, you wonder. What will she be like? It's like meeting a pen pal for the first time. You know about them, but you don't fully know them yet. You have yet to see them and experience them in person.

We entered the hospital room, and my mom was propped up in bed with this tiny bundle of blankets and a pink knit beanie barely visible on the top of Sarah's head. We each held her for a moment. I remember holding this little life in my arms. It was so surreal. Just a day ago, this baby was in my mom's stomach, and now she's sitting in my arms. A nurse came in the room. "Okay, big brothers, it's time for your beautiful little princess to get a few shots." Shots?! I thought. I hated getting shots. I couldn't imagine the nurse giving shots to this wonderful little life. Shots hurt. I know you need them, it's just … they hurt, really hurt! My dad led us into the hallway. The heavy wood door clicked shut, and then we heard Sarah let out a wail. I hated hearing that cry.

My dad reassured us she was going to be okay. He drove us to McDonald's to get some dinner. As I sat there looking at my burger and fries, I wondered what our life at home would be like now with another child to be taken care of. I was the youngest up to this point. Mom and Dad had what seemed like just enough love for Mike and me. Would they have enough love to share with another child? For that holiday season, McDonald's was selling small, stuffed Muppets. I asked my dad if we could get one for Sarah and take it back to her at the hospital. "Sure, son, we can get one, but we'll have to wait until tomorrow to give it to her," he said.

I picked out a small Kermit the Frog with a red Santa hat and scarf to match.

———————

Mary's life was about to change dramatically. The world she once knew would never be the same again. When God wants to do a great work in us, we begin to change the way we see the world around us. Our perspective begins to change. Mary could have said "no." She could have resisted, but God saw something in Mary and knew she would be faithful to carry, raise, and love His very own son.

So much of life is just like that. The opportunities, the relationships, the experiences, and the abilities are all gifts from God. He works in us. He gives to us the opportunity to steward with care each one of these moments. Think about your child. They are not yours to have and to hold forever. Yes, you are their parent, but they truly belong to God.

Think about the job you have. Yes, your skills and abilities landed you that job, but God is the one who gave you the skills to land the job in the first place. Your

home, possessions, and finances are, again, all yours—
to steward with care. When we boil it all down, we've
done nothing to earn or deserve anything we have. Everything is a gift from God. This mindset doesn't come
easily because we find so much of our identity and
worth in what we have, who we live with, and what
we do.

It's hard to understand. The truth is that, just as
quickly as we have received, we can lose those wonderful things in our lives. That's why it's so hard to
lose a loved one, a job, our ability to enjoy life when we
get sick or face a disappointment. We hurt when we are
at a loss. Until we understand it all belongs to God and
He's allowing us to get in on the enjoyment of life, we
will never truly know what it means to be alive.

Even the difficult situations we face are a gift from
God. Amid the pressure and tension, we grow as a
person. We learn to be thankful for all we have. Most
importantly, our faith and trust in God grow and develop. Our faith runs deep in difficult times.

This is the process of regaining a heart to believe
and trust. We learn about Jesus and Santa around the
same time. For many of us, in the stage of life we stop

believing in Santa, we also stop believing in Jesus. We can afford to stop believing in Santa (a little elf just stopped breathing), but we cannot afford to lose our belief in Jesus. The very things that cause us to forfeit our belief can also be the very catalysts that forge our belief in Jesus. It all comes down to a choice. Will I continue to see this difficult situation through? Can I find the good in this? What hope do I have of good to come?

Chapter Six

Peace of Patience

Do you remember what it was like to wait for Christmas morning? Do you remember the feeling of anticipation and excitement? Do you remember the wonder and waiting the night before? Do you remember the moment you saw the presents under the tree, how you tore open the colorful wrapping paper, and the moment you first laid eyes on the toy or gift you had longed for?

Those were the feelings that filled my world so many years ago one Christmas season. I was seven years old and the perfect age to fully comprehend all the good that the Christmas season brought: the lights, the songs, the smells, and the memories.

We had moved from our house on Phoenix Drive

just eleven months before. The previous Christmas, my sister had been born. This would be her very first Christmas. This would be our first Christmas in a new townhouse and new neighborhood, with new friends, making new memories.

The housing association for the development we lived in sent around flyers announcing a special Christmas decoration contest the week before Christmas. The townhomes were all rentals, and each home was connected in sections of five townhomes. The flyer stated that each section could decorate with a theme, lights, and displays, and the best decorated section would win a free month's rent.

My mom and dad collaborated with the other townhomes in our section. The young couple next door, whom we didn't see much, got on board and transformed their place into a winter wonderland. The house next to theirs belonged to close family friends of ours. They had two daughters, one Mike's age and one my age, and we all attended the same school. They chose to do a live nativity. The next neighbor was a middle-aged, divorced businessman whose daughter came every other weekend to visit. He dressed up as

Santa and had larger-than-life wrapped presents sitting on his lawn. The last house was a family of three. The couple had a son, but he was shy and never came out to play much. They decorated their place as Santa's workshop. And our place—I think we just covered every square inch of the shrubs with lights, placed candles in the windows, tacked red bows and greenery on each window sash, and hung a large beautiful wreath on the front door. We were going for a Martha Stewart/Better Homes and Gardens holiday look.

Each home had its distinct theme, with the main attraction of the live nativity. Mike played Joseph. Sarah was baby Jesus, with a Cabbage Patch stand-in if it got too cold. I had the option to be a shepherd, but I was too embarrassed to come out of the house in a bathrobe, flip-flops, and a bath towel on my head with a cinched brown belt for a headband.

The association sent representatives around the development to judge each section of homes. As soon as our section was judged, my dad loaded us up in the family station wagon and drove us around with small thermoses of hot chocolate to look at the lights and other displays in our neighborhood. We felt fairly confident we had a good display going. When we drove around the neighborhood, we only saw one other section of homes that would give us a little competition. The homes had all gone in on the same theme and recreated the North Pole. One home was a stable for the reindeer, another was Santa's workshop, and yet another was decorated like a candy shop and bakery you might find at Santa's place.

It was the kind of display a kid would love to explore and get lost in.

For the time being, we'd wait for the announcement of the winner. Meanwhile, our family finished up last-minute Christmas shopping. Mike and I celebrated the traditional Christmas party at school. We attended the annual Christmas Eve service at our church and came home to settle in for a "long winter's nap" the night before Christmas. We anxiously waited for the news. Would we be paying rent next month?

———————

We pick up the story with Mary making a trip to see her cousin Elizabeth. Was it her idea, her parent's idea, or Joseph's? We don't know for sure, but the trip to visit with family was fortuitous. Mary could get out from under the watchful and prying eyes of nosey neighbors and the gossip at synagogue. Mary traveled to the hill country of the city of Juda.

When she arrived, Mary entered Elizabeth and her husband Zacharias' house and said "Hello." It was more than just a "Hey, how are ya?" Luke records for us that Elizabeth's precious bundle of joy gave her a swift kick in the ribs. Elizabeth's response: "Mary, you are blessed and favored of the Lord. What did I do to deserve a visit from the one carrying our Lord?" Luke 1:39-43

Elizabeth confirmed the words of Gabriel. She gave Mary what no one else could, humanly speaking: the affirmation that she wasn't crazy. We all need that support in our lives.

There are times when we know God is doing something in us and around us. Imagine how Mary must have felt with these incredible words of blessing and goodness spoken over her. Too often in our lives, we speak words of correction only and neglect the opportunity to speak words of grace and confirmation of who God says we are as His children.

The message from God through Gabriel resounded in the words of Elizabeth. Mary could be sure that what was happening within her was an act of God.

There are five lessons we can learn from Mary's message and messengers from God.

1. Know God's words.

Mary grew up learning about the coming, promised Messiah. She heard the words of Gabriel shed more light on that very promise. She would hear of God's plan and purpose for her life from Elizabeth, as well —to be the mother of Jesus.

Sometimes we doubt what God is doing in our lives. If we would take but a moment and look to his word and promises, we would find comfort and confirmation that we are not without hope. We aren't crazy. We don't need to give up when things don't go according to plan.

2. Know God's works.

How does God work in the lives of people? What are the trends and patterns? We are all unique and different, yet God loves us and works with us in some very similar ways. Looking at the narratives of the Bible, we can gain some great insight into how God works and moves in our lives. So much of the Christmas story applies to our lives if we would but look for the little bread crumbs. Follow the stories of people who, in the face of difficulty and doubt, trusted God. Where did their trust lead them? You'll see a very clear connection between God's working and our waiting, just like we see in the life of Mary.

3. Know where to wait.

No doubt, Mary faced criticism. We can be sure her parents had to deal with questions such as these: Where is Mary? How long has she been gone? What's her time frame for coming back home—is it about nine months? Oh, she'll be coming home soon. Well, hasn't it been nine months since we've seen her? What about Joseph? What's he been up to? You can see where this is going.

Remember:

Some will criticize.

Some will condemn.

Some will correct.

... And some will encourage.

When you know God is working in your life, avoid the critics, drown out the condemners, forebear the correction, and embrace the encouragers. Elizabeth was the encourager and cheerleader Mary needed to patiently push on. We all need an Elizabeth in our life.

4. Know what to watch for.

Watch for God's confirmation of what he's doing in your life. As soon as Mary arrives, it is very clear she is doing the right thing by following God's purpose and plan for her life. How many of us have abandoned God's purpose because we had no vision for our future? We had no sign of God's stamp of approval. You don't need 100% of everyone's vote for you. You just need one or two people pulling for you. People who will travail with you through the process, and Elizabeth was just that person for Mary.

5. Know why you're waiting.

We don't get burned out because of what we do. We get burned out when we forget why we're doing what we're doing.

How can you stay encouraged in the waiting?

Journal. Write the thoughts you can't share with anyone else. Write the questions you have for God. Write your disappointments from yesterday and your hopes for tomorrow.

Talk. Share what you are going through with a friend, family member, or counselor. When we're trying to make sense of life and what we're going through, it's so helpful to have a second set of eyes on our situation. You don't have to talk to everybody. You just need to talk to somebody.

The message to each of us is this: be patient. When a dream is deferred, hope turns to hurt, a plan goes awry—be still. Listen to the message from God at the moment. Maybe God is asking you to be patient and watch Him unfold something glorious and wonderful before your eyes.

For our family that Christmas season, the glorious unfolding was a simple Christmas competition. It's just a little thing, a memory from a long time ago, but a treasure that has become part of the mosaic of my Christmas memories.

The week between Christmas and New Year, the association announced the winner. The section decorated like the North Pole and our section both won. We were so excited, but, looking back, my parents had to have been the most excited since they wouldn't have to pay a month's rent for our place!

Sometimes the littlest joys, words of encouragement, and glimpses of hope can be just the things to help us continue in the journey God has set before us.

Chapter Seven

A Message of Hope

I love my brother. I love Christmas music. I love Christmas music more than my brother loves Christmas music, and I'm to blame for that.

Mike is five years older than me. So much of how I view the world is due to the impact of an older brother. As a middle child, I have many of the tendencies explained in the parenting books. I like to mediate between people. I'm a "What do you want to do? I'm good, I'll do whatever you want to do" middle child. The only exception is when it comes to Christmas music.

Mike is a lover of oldies music. Growing up, we shared a room, a set of bunk beds, and a stereo. It wasn't just any stereo. It was an old Panasonic dual-cassette AM/FM radio and record player, with two wood-finish speakers the size of a two-drawer office filing cabinet. Most nights, we'd listen to the local oldies station out of Philadelphia: WOGL.

Everything derailed one Christmas season when I was cleaning out a hall closet to earn some extra spending money. I was in the basketball card-collecting phase I mentioned earlier. I pulled out some old leather coats that smelled a little too much like the cows had rolled around in the pasture pies and the stink had stuck with them. I pulled out several shoe boxes stacked behind the jackets. I sat on the floor of the hall and slipped the lid off the first gray and red shoebox. Inside, I found two rows of neatly packed cassette tapes. They all had green tape jackets with gold writing on them. I pulled out a tape from the middle of the bunch. It was a collection of Christmas songs. At the bottom of the tape jacket were the words "Volume 6." I pulled out another tape, "Volume 3," then another, "Volume 12."

I took the stash of tapes back to my room and dumped the whole set on my bed. I began putting the tapes in order. As I looked at each one, I noticed some of the volumes were classic Christmas hymns, others were more traditional carols, and some were from the era of

Bing Crosby and Nat King Cole. With each list of songs, I became more and more excited. Some of the songs I knew and was very familiar with; other songs I'd never even heard of. "Christmas in Killarney" and "Mele Kalikimaka" were just the beginning. Then I found it: "Dominick the Italian Christmas Donkey." That song changed Christmas for me forever.

I was in Christmas music heaven. That night before bed, Mike turned on WOGL to serenade us off to sleep. I asked if we could put in a tape instead. "Yeah, sure, no problem," Mike said. "What is it?" he asked. "You'll see. You'll love it. I know you will," I said.

Then came the sound of jingle bells jingling. A bassoon bounced in, and Lou Monte cheered, "Hey Jiggity, Jig- ..." Mike went along with it. We listened to Christmas songs late into the night, and I played a new volume each night from then on. I was good with it. Mike put up with it. The problem: we only had twelve volumes. I repeated cassette tapes over and over again until Christmas.

I think I ruined Christmas that year because my hall closet cleaning discovery happened in September. I made my brother listen to Christmas music for four months. He was a good sport and didn't complain. We were *really* in the Christmas spirit by the time it rolled around! It's funny because, today, my wife has a cardinal rule in our house: no Christmas music until the day after Thanksgiving. Some nights when I long for Christmas, I slip on a pair of headphones and cue up a Christmas playlist on Pandora. Amanda doesn't know. It's our secret.

———————

It's hard for me to think of a time when Christmas wasn't celebrated. It's hard for me to think of Joseph not knowing he would be memorialized on church front lawns, fireplace mantels, and dining room centerpieces as the tall central figure in the nativity display. Sometimes he's kneeling, other times he's standing, but he's always by Mary's side.

Joseph is portrayed as this stoic, strong, silent type. But was he? We know very little about this soon-to-be stepdad of Jesus. We know he was a carpenter. More likely, though, he would have worked with stone and likened more to our modern-day mason than a carpenter. The word used to describe Joseph was *tekton*, from which we get the words technical, technician, or technique. Joseph would have been an artisan or craftsman whose medium would have been stone, as homes and structures of that time were built with stone more often than wood.[1]

We know Joseph lived in Nazareth. We can assume he followed his father as an apprentice in the trade. We can also be fairly sure Joseph and Mary's families were close to one another socially—at least familiar enough for them to pursue an arranged married for their children.

Other than a reference to Joseph when Jesus is twelve and goes MIA on a family trip to Jerusalem, he's never spoken of again in the Gospels.

The gospel writer Matthew, a tax collector by trade, records for us Joseph's story. By virtue of his occupation, Matthew would have been a great record keeper. He begins his account of the life and times of Jesus by recording the genealogy of Jesus, via his stepdad Joseph, back to the throne of David. Matthew is writing to a Jewish audience. His goal is to corroborate and validate Jesus as the Messiah, the King of the Jews. After Matthew lays out the genealogy, he writes, "Now the birth of Jesus Christ was on this wise," or "Here's my secondhand account of Jesus' birth."

By the way, how would Matthew have known the story of Jesus' birth? All the gospel writers make note that Mary, Jesus' mother, was very much involved in the life and ministry of her son.

I'd imagine she was sitting down to a meal with the disciples one evening. Matthew sat next to her at the table and asked, "So, Mary, how did all of this begin?" The story of Jesus' birth was beyond mythology or folklore shared around campfires. The birth of Jesus would have been on par with the miraculous accounts of his ministry in Galilee and Judea, his death on the cross, and his resurrection from the grave.

We pick up again with Matthew's account as he shares with us a more bullet-point, fact-by-fact account of Joseph's story. We'll get into the depth of Joseph's take on the Christmas story, but as you'll soon find out—no spoiler alert needed—Joseph was about to dive headlong into a sticky situation.

In a matter of moments, Joseph finds out his wife-to-be is pregnant, and the child is not his. What's a guy to do?

Have you ever found yourself in a sticky, messy, possibly embarrassing situation like Joseph's? He's getting advice from all sides. Who does he side with? Who does he take a side against?

When faced with a difficult decision, we have a choice: take a side or take a stand. One response is passive. The other response is active.

Joseph's choices were to take a side and keep his reputation or take a stand and save his relationship with Mary.

If Joseph had taken a side, he would have erased himself completely out of the Christmas story. There would be a void in the nativity display, and we'd be looking to change some Christmas carols.

Has the temptation to succumb to popular opinion ever forced you to take a side? Did the sense of disappointment, rejection, and disapproval become just too much to bear? Could you be missing out on being a part of some of the most incredible miracles of God because you took a side instead of taking a stand?

Chapter Eight

Joseph's Stand

The wind blew hard and cold as I walked from my dorm to the music building on campus. I was a sophomore in college in West Virginia. My nightly routine was starting. Dinner was served from 5:00 to 6:30 p.m. I had dinner, talked with friends in the college cafeteria, and then headed back to the dorm to grab my bag. I was a voice major in the music program. Why? I had sung in junior high and high school. I didn't like the program I was in my freshman year of college, so I transferred to the music program as a voice major and a minor in piano. What would a degree in music get me after graduation? Most likely a stint as a singing telegram or a back-up singer on one of those reality TV song shows. Maybe a worship leader in a church. Who knew? I was confused and unsure of what my future held.

Dr. Suiter was my course advisor, choral-conducting teacher, voice coach, and mentor. My attempt at being a music major wasn't going so well. For the choral conducting class, we had to conduct a passage from Handel's holiday classic, *Messiah*. As a part of the class, we had to use a video camera to record ourselves conducting a portion of music. I had to conduct the song as if I were standing before a full choir, complete with a symphony orchestra, when actually the room was empty except for Dr. Suiter, me, and two other students taking the class. It was my turn, and all I can say is that it was a train wreck. Dr. Suiter gave me a chance to try it again a second time, then told me to watch the video footage and make adjustments. He would give me another chance the following week. I reviewed the footage. I looked like a blind mime duck hunting in a snowstorm. It didn't go well.

As I walked to the music building, I was not feeling it. I wasn't in the mood to be conducting Handel's *Messiah*. I wasn't in the mood to be in college at the time. I had no money and, worse yet, no purpose. I had broken up with a girl. I was floundering. To top it all off, Dr. Suiter asked me to sing a solo piece for the college Christmas concert just before we stopped classes for Christmas break. The song he gave me to sing wasn't my jam: "Jacob's Star." It wasn't a Christmas carol. It wasn't even a familiar Christmas song. I hated it, but as part of my course requirements, I had to practice voice exercises and performance songs one to two hours each day for our recital at the end of the semester. One of the songs was "Jacob's Star." Dr. Suiter was big into not only being technically correct with a song but also hitting the right notes and pronouncing each word correctly. He wanted his voice students to feel the song and communicate the emotion. He wanted us to use the song to connect with the crowd.

I wasn't feeling it, even though I was hitting the notes and singing with correct diction. My heart was as far away as possible, and he could tell. He stopped me during my session with him. "Matt, later tonight when you work on this song, I want you to imagine yourself as Joseph singing this song. Imagine what it must have been like to know the pressure and uncertainty of being betrothed. Think of the difficulty of the long journey from Nazareth to Bethlehem. What would you smell, hear, and feel that night holding Jesus in your arms for the very first time? That's what I want to hear. I don't want to hear the right notes and perfect enunciation. I want to feel what Joseph felt. The audience won't be able to feel that unless you feel that. Your job is to make us care, make us feel, take us back to the quiet of the stable, to the wonder, awe, and intimacy of the moment. Capture that moment, and this will be a concert we will never forget."

Just capture the moment. How in the world was I supposed to do that?

I walked into the darkness of the entryway to the music building. The hall lights were on a sensor and came to life as soon as I stepped into the hallway. I wound my way through the building to the practice rooms. I pulled open a door to the small seven-by-ten-foot room and flipped on the light. There was an upright piano, bench, mirror, and small chair in the corner. I set my stuff down, pulled out my tape recorder, cued up the song I was about to karaoke to and tried to imagine what it would have been like for Joseph two thousand years ago.

Joseph was in a pickle. This was no pickle like the pickle Benny "the Jet" Rodriguez faced in *The Sandlot*. This was a situation in which there was no way to make everyone happy. Somebody was going to lose. Someone was not going to be happy.

Matthew tells us that Mary was pregnant before she and Joseph had ever come together to be married officially. He describes Joseph as a just man who didn't want to make a public example of her but to divorce her privately.

We must pull back the curtain on Jewish law, culture, and tradition to understand what's going on here.

According to Jewish law in the Torah (the first five books of the Old Testament, specifically Leviticus and Deuteronomy), when a Jewish couple was betrothed to be married, they would officially be "off the market" for marriage to anyone else. While they would not yet begin living together, the dowry was set, the fathers would negotiate the price, and the couple would begin preparations for the wedding day. The husband would begin to build a home for his new family, and the wife-to-be would prepare herself as well. When the construction of the house was completed, the groom would gather his bridal party, make a big procession to his betrothed's home, and lead her to the marriage feast.

Even though the couple was officially committed to one another, they refrained from consummating the marriage until after the wedding feast. Infidelity at this juncture would be on par with adultery. In Jewish law, adultery was punishable, and the punishment was death by stoning. It was a part of their culture in that day. The Jews would make it a very public example as a warning to anyone with less than the purest intentions to get married.

The other option Joseph had was to divorce her privately. They had not been physically intimate or started a family. They hadn't even begun living together. He could save face and start over. The story for Mary, on the other hand, didn't look as promising. She would most likely be forced to stay single or marry someone with less than honorable intentions.

Here were Joseph's options:

1. Publicly divorce Mary. This would save his reputation. You can imagine the implications for Mary, her family, and her future—she had none. Joseph would lose Mary and potentially cause a problem for God's plan. I don't think we can go there mentally with the implications of this scenario, but you get the idea.

2. Privately divorce Mary. This would, more or less, save his reputation—but not necessarily with the most devout Jews who knew the truth of the matter. He would ultimately lose his relationship with Mary. She would end up raising Jesus as a single mom and hope to find someone to marry her at some point.

When you think you only have two options, always look for another option.

Joseph's third option: Marry Mary. Joseph would most surely lose his reputation. He would lose his credibility and possibly his business. But he would save his relationship with Mary and his opportunity to guide, mentor, protect, raise, and love Jesus.

While God's message to Mary was "be patient," God's message to Joseph was "be faithful."

It's when you want to give up, choose the path of least resistance, and side with the most popular opinion that God asks you to stand and be faithful. If Joseph hadn't stood by Mary's side so long ago, the Christmas nativity would look much different.

Chapter Nine

An Undeniable Choice

Silence can be unsettling. The music building was quiet and still that night. I was alone in my little world in a big building in the middle of the hills of West Virginia. God meets us in the strangest and most unassuming of places. God met me in that little practice room that night.

As I played the song and sang the lyrics over and over again, something began to settle into my soul.

A fire, a light, a shining star,

A sign to those who journeyed far,

A token from the king of heaven,

A spark as to the light of the world.

A beacon burning in the night,

A star to echo endless light,

A darkened world, a light from a stable

And high above the heavens ablaze.

A Star will rise from Jacob's house.

The words are a poetic expression of an Old Testament prophecy:

I shall see him, but not now: I shall behold him, but not nigh: there shall come a Star out of Jacob, and a Scepter shall rise out of Israel, and shall smite the corners of Moab, and destroy all the children of Sheth (Numbers 24:17 KJV).

These words were a part of the Torah which both Mary and Joseph would have memorized at synagogue at a young age.

The words began to click. The promise of God to his people was going to be fulfilled. What's interesting is that the prophecy is dual in that a Star, a Messiah, would come to save His people. He would be from the line of Jacob. As the verse tells us, this one to rise from Jacob's house would also bring freedom and victory over those who would fight and oppose the people of God.

For the keen students of the Torah, Joseph would

have looked at this verse and wondered if this Messiah to be born of Mary would be the one to deliver them from the iron rule of the Romans. The first part of the prophecy was fulfilled when Jesus was born that cool night so long ago. The problem was that his fulfillment of the second prophecy is still to come.

The best way to describe the prophecy would be looking at the form of a mountain from miles away. What you see before you appears to be one massive mountain. The closer you get to the mountain, though, you realize it's not one but two mountains. This is what the prophets saw in Jesus. This is what would unfold before Joseph.

What I saw unfolding in my life and my journey was that God was guiding me. I was confused as to God's calling in my life. I didn't sense from God that college was the right place for me. I was called to encourage, inspire, and share Jesus with people. But was this the place God had for me to follow that calling? Or should I give up the calling altogether? The music thing wasn't working out. Should I pack my bags and go home?

I sang the song over a final time. In the stillness and quietness of the practice room, late that night in early

December, I sense in my spirit God telling me, "Your time here is over, but my work in your life is just beginning."

I can remember praying that night, "God you've promised to lead me and guide me. You've promised that the work you've begun in me you will finish in me. I've followed you. I've done what I thought you wanted me to do, but now it seems like plans are changing. But, if you are moving me on to another phase and another stage of life, I'll follow what you want me to do."

The call to my parents was one more step of confirmation that my time in West Virginia was over. The next place was yet to be discovered. I decided, in those days leading to the end of the fall semester of my sophomore year of college, that it was the end of that season of life. I was heartbroken, but the turmoil and indecision gave way to peace in my heart.

Just before we parted for Christmas break, the Christmas concert would be my final contribution to the place I had called home for eighteen months.

The night of the concert came. I was dressed in a black tuxedo, and I had warmed up backstage with Dr. Suiter. I looked over the program guide for the evening, and there was my name halfway down the second page: "'Jacob's Star'......Matt Manney." I had committed, and there was no turning back.

"Matt, just remember what you have worked on. You know the notes. You know the words. Now communicate the message. Make us feel what you feel. Make us feel what Joseph felt."

It was my turn to take center stage. The concert hall was dark except for dim lights lining the exterior aisles. I could barely make out the silhouettes of the faces in the crowd. The spotlight came on, and Dr. Suiter sat at the piano and began playing.

My mind began to replay all the memories from my time in this place. My long nights in music practice rooms. Dinner with friends in the cafeteria. Talking late into the night about hopes and dreams in college dorm rooms. Sitting around campfires and sharing stories of what God was doing in our lives with the rest of the student body. Then the meeting with the college vice president, who tried to get me to stay. I was vacating my position as the sophomore class president, the role I played as the leader of a singing team that traveled for the college on the weekends, and my service as president of the missionary prayer band. Why in the world was I walking away from all of this?

As I looked out and sang the words to "Jacob's Star," I sensed, with every beat and measure sung, God confirming and reassuring in my soul, "This is it. It's time for you to move on and follow my leading."

The decision made little sense to anyone at the college, but I had the counsel and confirmation of my parents, pastor, and most importantly, from God.

I hit the last two phrases:

> *A light the world has not comprehended.*
> *A light that is this holy babe.*

The last few notes of the piano echoed through the hall. There was silence, then a round of applause. It was as though God himself were applauding. "Well done, my son. This is the last of your journey in this place."

———

Joseph thought deeply about his choices. We know he did because Matthew tells us in the twentieth verse of the first chapter. God was about to send a message so clear that there would be no denying what Joseph should do.

You will find yourself at times in your life when, out of nowhere, God will reveal his plan and purpose for you. His direction will be undeniable. His peace will permeate you. His love will guide you. For Joseph, the message would come from a familiar face to us. Gabriel was about to visit Joseph, as well.

Chapter Ten

Prophecy of Peace

What would it take to create an angel? You'd need a white bedsheet, a strip of white construction paper, tape, and lots of gold-tinsel pipe cleaner. The bedsheet would be the angel's robe; the gold pipe cleaner would be the halo. If you were fancy, you might try to fashion a set of wings out of a wire clothes hanger and white stockings.

What would it take to have a dream of an angel? For us, it might take a late-night cheesy stuffed-crust pizza with olives, anchovies, maybe a little roasted red pepper—and two Tums, just in case. You would have all kinds of wonderful dreams on a stomach full of that late-night snack.

In Joseph's case, Matthew tells us he was thinking

about what to do for Mary just before he pillowed his head. Some psychologists say that if you want to solve a problem and work on it in your sleep, let the problem be the last thought on your mind as you drift off into la-la-land.

Joseph's answer would be in the form of an angel of the Lord coming to him in a dream.

The conversation goes:

> "Joseph, don't be afraid to marry Mary. What's been conceived in her is a miracle of the Holy Ghost. It's a God thing. She will bring forth a son, and you'll call him Jesus because he will save his people from their sins."[1]

Matthew gives us an editorial: "This was all done to fulfill the prophecy of Isaiah stating, 'a virgin would conceive, a son as a matter of fact, and his name will be Emmanuel, which means God with us.'"[2] There are a few insights we can gather from the message from the angel and the additional information from Matthew.

The prophecy was a reference from the prophet Isaiah's writings. Joseph would have been familiar with these words, as they were spoken of and read about in synagogue. The words spoken by the angel would have rung true in Joseph's mind.

The imperative for Joseph to call the baby Jesus comes from Jewish tradition. The father was traditionally the one to officially name a child. Any father would most likely consult with his wife, but he was the one who gave the name and identity to his child at birth. This was a semblance of a blessing and proclamation of who the child was to the parents. Many times, the father would name the child after himself, as a junior, or another member of the family.

Mary's cousin Elizabeth and her husband Zacharias were tasked with this same challenge. Zacharias was a priest fulfilling his routine duties in the temple when the angel Gabriel appeared to him and told him to call his newborn son John. Zacharias didn't believe Gabriel. As a sign of how serious Gabriel was, he took away Zacharias' ability to speak.

When the child was born nine months later, the family asked Elizabeth what she and her husband would name the baby. She told them "John." They were shocked. They thought he would be named after his father or another member of the family. No one in the family was named John. The family asked Zacharias what he thought. He called for a tablet and wrote the letters J-O-H-N. "His name is to be John." As soon as he wrote this, he regained his ability to speak.

Joseph would find a similar task before him. Why "Jesus"? In Hebrew, the name is Joshua. In Greek, we have Jesus. Both names mean "God is my salvation." His name reflected his purpose: he would save his people from their sins.

Then we have this interesting mention of another name taken from Isaiah 7:14: "A virgin shall conceive and bear a son, and shall call his name Emmanuel."

Jesus has many names we find throughout the New Testament. His name mentioned by Matthew is a connection and fulfillment of Isaiah's prophecy seven hundred years before his birth. Not only was he "God is my salvation," but he was also "God is with us."

God had not revealed himself to the Jews for four hundred years. Jesus' arrival on the scene was the fulfillment of a long-hoped-for promise. God's reputation was on the line with the Jews, and their faith and trust in him were waning. We'll see this come into play later in the story.

Joseph's dream was more than prophecies and proclamations of good to come. It was the promise that God had planned to bring calm out of the chaos.

Maybe you're facing a chaotic situation right now. You struggle to make sense of your situation. How does a 700-year-old prophecy, a confused soon-to-be-married masonry worker, and a pizza-induced dream help your case? I'm glad you asked.

Joseph's dream reminds us that God cares about us. The problem Jesus was coming to fix was not just a problem for the Jews. It is a problem for all of us. We have a problem called sin that keeps us from connecting with God and knowing Him as our father.

The prophecy means God cares. The prophecy means God hasn't forgotten his people. It means God hasn't forgotten you.

If God can make good on a seven-hundred-year-old prophecy through the birth of a baby in a stable over two thousand years ago, God can make good on his promises to us. Jesus tells us about his Father, that he has provided for us. Jesus tells us of himself, that he will never leave us or forsake us because of the Holy Spirit who has come to be our Comforter.

Don't get lost in the prophecy and miss the promise. God loves you. God is for you. God is in you. God is with you.

Chapter Eleven

Being Faithful

The lights, music, and moment were so magical, I wished I could capture it in a bottle. Have you ever had moments like that? Have you had moments when you felt like you were in the middle of a movie, everything seemed so perfect and just right?

Victoria Gardens was beautiful that December night in 2005. Amanda was even more beautiful. It had been three years since my swan song that cold December night at college in West Virginia. The new season of life brought new friendships, new opportunities, and new hopes and dreams.

I enrolled at a small Bible college in Southern California. On the weekends, I volunteered to be on a team of college students who started a small chapel an hour north of the college in Mojave, a little town of about three thousand people smack dab in the middle of the Mojave Desert.

I met Amanda on that team. She played the piano for church services, and I led the worship. Our friends on the team, Ronnie and Jen, were getting married that December. Justin, Jaime, another Jen, Amanda, and I drove south from the college to Oceanside, California to attend the wedding.

Amanda and I had been dating for ten months at that point, and I knew I wanted to marry her. Our relationship was a new lease on life for me. It was the renewed hope from the wondering and doubt I had struggled with while I was living in West Virginia.

The wedding was great. We laughed, cheered, and sent Ronnie and Jen off in a fanfare of bubbles and well wishes. On the drive back to college, we decided to stop at Victoria Gardens. The outdoor mall had just opened a year before. Christmas trees, lights, music—and love—filled the cool night air, at least for Amanda and me. We walked around the mall and window shopped. We stopped by a coffee shop and grabbed a caramel vanilla latte to share. We laughed with our friends. We talked about our plans for Christmas. We talked about Ronnie and Jen's wedding and about what a wedding would look like for us if that were something God had in store.

We had become fast friends in those ten months. I knew Amanda was the one I wanted to spend the rest of my life with. How sure was I about that? I was sure enough that I had called her dad a few months before the wedding and asked him if I could marry his daughter. He said, "Go for it!" I purchased an engagement ring and kept it with me everywhere I went. I didn't necessarily think an opportunity would present itself to propose; I just didn't want to leave it out of my sight.

That night, walking through Victoria Gardens, we took pictures in front of a gorgeous Christmas tree and talked more about what a wedding would look like for us. Amanda said, "I think I would love a wedding around Christmas, but the timing would never work."

"What do you mean?" I asked.

"Well, you graduate in the spring. I won't graduate until next December. The wedding would have to be at least a year and a half from now. What do you think?" she asked.

"I don't know. How long does it take to plan a wedding?" I had no clue. I was hoping something simple and quick. "What, like a couple of weeks, right?" I said.

She laughed. "No, Babe, it would take more like a year."

At the moment I wondered, *Did I jump the gun on the ring?* What Amanda didn't know was that the whole time we were talking, I had the ring in a small box deep in the side pocket of my leather jacket. I was holding it the whole time we talked.

"I don't know. I guess we'll just have to wait and see," I told her.

I didn't know when to "pop" the question, but I knew without a doubt I wanted to do life with this woman. I wanted to pursue our dreams together, raise kids with her, and grow old together, really old.

In only three weeks, I would know the answer to my question of when to ask Amanda to marry me. The next question, though, was would she say yes?

———

Joseph awakes from his dream from Gabriel. (Just a

side note: if you have a dream and see someone who looks like an angel, better be ready to have a baby. Gabriel was like a celestial stork delivering babies, just ... minus the baby.)

He goes to Mary. "I know you're telling the truth. I believe this baby-to-be is from God."

"What do you mean, Joseph?" Mary asks.

"I mean that I had a dream and Gabriel told me to not be afraid to marry you. He told me to call our baby Jesus. I believe you. I don't know what all this means. For now, we need to get ready for this baby."

Can you imagine the peace, the relief, the smile of joy, and the feeling of love? Joseph chose to marry Mary. He was committing to this life of leading and raising the Son of God. He was stepping up to the plate to be Jesus' stepdad. Do you see what's unfolding? Even Jesus knows what it means to be in a blended family. Joseph's character and integrity shine through. Matthew even indicates in his account that Joseph chose to wait until after Jesus was born to sleep with Mary. He fulfilled his part, and when the baby was born, he named him Jesus.

What was the calling for Joseph? What part was he

to play in the Christmas story? He simply had to show up, commit to caring for Mary, and protect this baby from birth to adulthood. Joseph had to be faithful.

Sometimes the most glorious and noteworthy thing we can do is show up and be faithful. As easy as that sounds, there is a lot that goes into making that happen. If we can be faithful to show up in our marriage, our family, our friendships, and our workplace, how would that change our lives?

It's simple but tough. The challenge is three-fold.

1. Be present in the moment with the people in our lives who matter most.

2. Stay focused on the purpose set before us.

3. Disregard the distractions of others that would get us off track.

Joseph would do the miraculous. He would claim his place in history not as a flashy, glorious hero. He would take a backstage roll in this production. But he was crucial to the story. Without Joseph, there would be no Christmas story.

You may feel as if your life doesn't matter. You may feel as if no one cares about you, for you, or even acknowledges your contributions. When you feel that way, don't forget that God knows and God cares. Be faithful to God, and you will begin to see where you matter most and who you matter most to.

Chapter Twelve

The Courage to Stand

There are some gifts you can give that will not cost you money. These gifts cannot be wrapped up and placed under a tree. They do have a price tag. They are simple gifts that cost you the investment of time, energy, care, and love. The person you bestow these gifts upon, if they are watchful and careful, will truly see the incredible value of the gift you have given.

Joseph took a stand on behalf of Mary. His decision to marry her was a direct contradiction of the counsel he was given. He could potentially lose his reputation with the naysayers in the short term. In the long-term, he would gain credibility with God.

When you want to give people the gift of yourself as Joseph gave to Mary, here are some thoughts to keep in mind.

1. Give the gift of a good reputation.

The reputation you want tomorrow you choose today.
Joseph's choice was about to go public.

We don't know for sure, but we can assume that
Mary spent most of her pregnancy with Elizabeth in
Juda. By the time she comes back, God uses the natural
course of life and a little bit of prophetic fulfillment to
take them away from the gossip and leering eyes of on-
lookers in Nazareth. Caesar Augustus would call for a
census, meaning Joseph and Mary would have to travel to Bethlehem when she was nine months pregnant.

2. Give the gift of waiting wisdom.

When you think you only have two options, wisdom
waits for a third option. What if Joseph had been de-
cisive, impulsive, and impatient? What if he would
have decided to publicly or privately divorce Mary?
Because he waited and pondered his dilemma, he gave
God room to work and send the news from Gabriel.

I wonder sometimes how our lives would look if we
slowed things down, took a breath, and waited for God

to reveal the natural next step. I wonder if the quality of our decisions and the wisdom we use to make those decisions would improve.

3. Give the gift of loyalty.

Stand in response to Jesus' teachings, values, and principles. We have a choice as to the basis upon which we make our decisions:

> 1. Our decisions reflect our family or societal norms.
>
> 2. Our decisions reject our family or societal norms.
>
> 3. Our decisions project Jesus' new way of living. We love God. We love our neighbors. We love our enemies.

The third decision is in total opposition to the first two ways of decision making. When we are loyal to Jesus, he shows who and how to stand for what is right in his sight. Mary needed someone to stand with her, to be her advocate, guide, and protector. Everyone needs that kind of person in their life. People long for loyalty more than we could ever know.

4. Give the gift of courage.

Faithful isn't glamorous. It's not flashy. It's not trendy. But faithful is fearless. There are so many distractions, expectations, and suspicions that can capsize our capacity to be faithful. It takes courage to stick with someone or something. The ability to be faithful when things are going well, people are easy to love, and the sun is shining is no big thing. Change that scenario to dealing with difficult situations, difficult people, and rainy days, and we've got an entirely different challenge to being faithful.

Courage is best expressed not in being fearless but in doing what is right even when things are fearful, uncertain, and uncomfortable.

5. Give the gift of trust.

God's overarching prophecy and promise to the Jews was unfolding in the lives of a young couple on the eve of their wedding. For so many years, the people of Israel had been waiting for God to break through the silence and into their pain. Did God care? Could they trust Jehovah?

Joseph played a role in being engaged to Mary in

this story. He was faced with a crisis. He had been given an "out" (according to the Jewish customs of his day he could have divorced Mary) and could have easily not gone along with the miraculous work God was doing. He chose to keep his word and follow through with his commitment to marry Mary.

There will be times when we are faced with a crisis. We will have the opportunity to bow out, save face, and save ourselves from a headache and heartache. In those moments, our ability to follow through even when we don't have to will reveal our credibility and trust. Joseph chose his relationship with Mary over his reputation. Ladies, does that sound like the kind of man you'd like to marry? With each revelation of Matthew's account, we realize why Joseph was a part of this incredible Christmas story.

6. Give the gift of goodness.

Stand for good, and God will get the glory. Look for glamour, and you're out of the story. How many times have we written ourselves out of the story? We got discouraged, confused, or frustrated. Things weren't going according to plan or moving along as we had hoped. So, we bailed. We threw in the towel and got out of the fray.

The writer of Hebrews tells us Jesus is writing our story of faith. If we can trust what God is doing in our lives, even when it doesn't make sense, we can see what He is doing is for His glory and our good. There may be things we won't understand until we get to heaven, but with time we can learn to trust and praise God.

———————

Being faithful is not a matter of being right or being wrong. Faithfulness is putting the priority of our relationships and commitment to Jesus over our reputation.

When you don't know which side to take, take a stand with Jesus and the people you love. Follow Joseph and be faithful.

Chapter Thirteen

Timely Interruptions

The garage door slid down the track and locked into place. The lights in the garage bays were turned off. The OPEN sign flipped to CLOSED.

"Hey Tom, I'll see you tomorrow. We working a full day?" my uncle asked.

"No, just until four o'clock. We've got the service at church for Christmas Eve," my dad said.

"You heading home before this snow gets any worse?" Bruce asked.

"That's my plan," my dad said.

The phone on the desk in the office of my dad's auto repair shop rang. "Hello," my dad answered. "Hi, Sweetheart. How's it going?" my mom asked.

"Good, Honey. I'm just locking up. I've sent all the

guys home before the snow gets too bad," he said.

"Did you have a chance to get to the toy store this afternoon?" he asked my mom.

"No, I didn't get a chance to get away after the boys came home from school," she said.

My dad looked out the front window of the shop. The snow was coming down hard. The gas pumps and cars in the lot had a coating of white covering them like icing on a cake. He dropped his shoulders.

"What's tomorrow look like?" he asked.

"We've got the Christmas Eve Service at five o'clock," she said. "Why don't you come home? This weather is too bad. I don't want you to get into a car accident. We'll figure out what to do for the boys to-morrow," she said.

"It's okay. I don't want you to have to worry about it," my dad said.

"Tom, please come home. I don't want you to be out in this weather. Plus, will the stores still be open?"

"I'll take the tow truck. I'll be fine," my dad said. "I'll be home in an hour."

My dad turned out the lights in the office and began to think through a plan.

If I grab a cup of coffee, I'll be able to make it to Toys "R" Us before they close. And I'm looking for a construction set for each of the boys.

That year, the toy industry didn't set parents up to succeed. Publicity stunts were all the rage. Companies were keeping parents' supply and demand needs at a fever pitch. Dropping Cabbage Patch dolls from helicopters wasn't too far-fetched.

The plan was to drive to the toy store and pick up a LEGO set for Matthew and a construction set for Michael. My dad loaded up his bag of paperwork and a travel mug of coffee in the cab of the tow truck. The steam from the hot coffee swirled into the air, mingling with the smell of grease, oil, and gasoline. The engine roared to life, and my dad pulled out of the snow-covered lot onto the snow-covered street. Only a car or two passed by slowly in the slush. A plow truck passed, trying to keep up with the snowfall.

December 23rd—Christmas Eve eve. This was not the time to be out doing last-minute shopping. This was like a scene out of *Jingle All the Way*. My dad drove the twenty-minute trip in forty minutes, with the conditions decreasing visibility. He passed the massive

King of Prussia Mall with its parking lot sitting empty. *I hope Toys "R" Us is still open,* he thought. The tow truck came to a stop in the parking lot. Only a few cars could be seen, most likely those of employees. He pulled the door of the store open and began the dreaded search for the perfect toy, the coveted construction sets.

Store shelves were empty except for the knock-off, want-to-be toys that were like the real thing but not name brand. "Where's the LEGO set aisle?" he asked an employee. "Oh, sir, we're all sold out. And just to let you know, we'll be closing in fifteen minutes because of the snow," the kid behind the register said.

He perused through one toy aisle to the next. *What am I going to get the boys?* Then, like the shining light of the Holy Grail, there was one last construction set sitting on the shelf. *An Erector set. Perfect!* he thought. *It's not exactly what he wanted, but I had one as a kid. Michael will love this.* On the way back out of the aisle, he saw a Lincoln Log set. *It's not LEGO, but it has interlocking pieces. I'm sure Matthew will like it.* The last-minute, eleventh hour trip to the toy store was a success. Or was it?

Interruptions are no fun. Stress. Pressure. Expectations. Empty toy shelves. These don't make for a very happy holiday. The job of a parent is to deliver because Santa Claus sure isn't going to. How do we handle life's little and big interruptions? We can get stressed, frustrated, maybe even irritated. Interruptions can keep us from enjoying the most wonderful time of the year. Maybe it's bad news from the doctor's visit. Your child's teacher shared at the parent-teacher meeting that your kiddo is falling behind the rest of the class. You never got the call back from the girl. You thought the date went well, but now she's ghosted you. Maybe she's auditioning for a part in *A Christmas Carol*? We have plans. We have hopes. We have interruptions that can turn into disappointments. These disappointments can set us up for a major let down, especially around the holidays. We think, *It's not supposed to be this way!*

Interruptions can be a gift, though. They can keep us from going in a direction in life we shouldn't. Interruptions can be God's hand working in us to chip away a part that's keeping us from growing. Interruptions can be simply God's gift to show us where He is working. He wants to give us a ringside seat to the miracles he is doing. The only way to get our attention and snap us out of our target fixation is none other than an interruption.

The shepherds were no different than you and I. They were blue-collar workers just trying to make a living. That was all about to change one starry night on a hillside overlooking a little town called Bethlehem.

Chapter Fourteen

Unexpected Invitation

The snow eased up. My dad pulled into the driveway on Phoenix Drive. The Erector set and Lincoln Logs were perfect-sized gifts. The construction sets came in boxes the size of a large sheet cake and would look great under the tree wrapped in bright, colorful paper.

He sneaked the large white shopping bags, with TOYS "R" US conspicuously printed on the sides in colorful block lettering, into the large walk-in closet in my parents' bedroom.

Christmas Eve came and went. My folks wrapped the presents and couldn't wait to see our eyes light up the following morning.

I should have made it a little easier on my parents that Christmas. Things got off to a rough start when both Mike and I unwrapped socks and underwear, one pack after another—Mom had hit a sale at the local department store. We each got a couple of VHS tapes. Mike got a copy of *Back to the Future* Part 1 and Part 2, while I opened a copy of *The Karate Kid* Part II and *An American Tail*.

Anticipation was building. The presents up to this point were okay. There were still two large presents tucked under the tree. "Okay boys, here are your last big presents," my mom said.

Mike opened his. I opened mine. Silence. "What is this?" Mike asked. "It's called an Erector set. You'll love it. I had one when I was a kid," my dad explained. "Do you like the Lincoln Logs, Matthew?" my mom asked. "I asked for a LEGO set," I said. "I wanted a different construction set," Mike said.

If this Christmas would have been in another century, I probably wouldn't be alive to tell the story. Kids can be short-sighted and ungrateful. Sure, there's disappointment, but we learned an important lesson that year: be grateful for what you have. We had no idea what our parents were going through that Christmas. We wouldn't know until we were adults what those construction sets represented.

Untimely interruptions can be divine intervention, God's attempt to get our attention.

Imagine that evening when the shepherds had finally settled in for the night. They had the sheep counted and secured in the fold. The shepherds may have used a cave or, more likely, a make-shift wall of stacked stone to create the fold. They may have intertwined briars, thorns, and brush and placed them on top as a sort of barbed wire for a defense against wild animals or thieves who might want to steal the sheep. That night, they would likely have had a fire going to cook their evening meal and take a little chill out of the air. One shepherd may have taken the first watch overseeing the entrance to the fold.

Have you ever been asleep when someone mistakenly comes into the room and flips the light switch on? The immediate sensation of bright light can throw your corneas into a spasm. Imagine the fear that struck their hearts when the angel first appeared on that night so long ago.

———————

Mary and Joseph had made the ninety-mile trek from Nazareth to Bethlehem. As the story goes, they couldn't find any place to stay. This could have been due to the number of people who had come to town to pay taxes and be counted for the census. The mandate from Caesar was for the people to be accounted for in the town of their heritage. With Joseph's lineage going back to David, and Bethlehem David's hometown, Bethlehem was going to be the place to find refuge for the night until they could pay their tax and be counted.

With Mary nine months pregnant, it was surprising no one had enough pity on the young couple to make space for them. Was this because people knew about the scandal? Were they just hard-hearted to the needs of a young mom? We don't know. What we do know is that at least one innkeeper made space in the garage for them. In their day, you put your transportation in a stable or barnyard for safekeeping through the night. The hills of Bethlehem were made of a soft limestone, so a cave could easily be carved out of the side of a hill with the home backing up into the hill. Some homes were constructed like a bi-level home, with the living space on the top floor and the stable for the animals on the ground floor. Either way, it was not a place to have a baby. The ideal place would be a home or even a palace, like the one Herod built only a stone's throw from Bethlehem.

As Mary and Joseph settled into their humble living quarters for the night and prepared for a little visitor to be born, a group of shepherds were getting a visitor of their own.

The shock and terror they felt is described by Luke as "sore afraid."[1] They were so fearful it was painful. This visit was more than an interruption—it was a frightful moment. It's in the frightful moments of life that we can begin to see the faithful movements of God. Was God trying to scare them, punish them, taunt them, or flex his power? God was coming to tell them something they were not going to want to miss.

We'll see in the chapters to come how different people respond to the news of a baby born in Bethlehem. The religious leaders knew the prophecies. Wise men were about to travel from the east, led by a star. A king was about to throw a big temper tantrum.

The shepherds were valued by God enough to have a personal invitation to the greatest single event in human history up to this point.

What is God inviting you to? What if the interruption could be more than frustration and irritation for us? What if the interruption is an invitation for us to see something God has just for us? Are you watching? Are you willing to see? Are you willing to be interrupted?

Chapter Fifteen

Glorious Unfolding

Confusion. Fear. Bright light.

As teenagers, we would play a horrible prank on each other at sleepovers. The unsuspecting victim was whoever fell asleep first. We would grab a thick, heavy down pillow and a flashlight. We'd sneak up as quiet as possible to the guy sleeping soundly. One guy stood with the pillow high over his head ready to swing. Another guy held the flashlight just an inch or two from the closed eyes of our unsuspecting victim. Then, without warning, the flashlight would click on, we'd shout "TRAIN," and the guy with the pillow would swing square at Sleeping Beauty's forehead.

There were no pranks on the night Jesus was born. The angelic host was the real deal. No lighting effects.

No dry ice and fog machines. This was God coming down from on high after a four-hundred-year sabbatical of silence. God was about to break onto the scene of humanity once more, but this time He would do so in a way unlike any other visitation.

The fateful, ungrateful Christmas morning of unwanted socks, underwear, Erector sets, and Lincoln Logs was the sign of something deeper going on in our family. My parents were stressed. My dad's business wasn't doing well. People weren't paying their repair bills to get their cars fixed. The company that sold gas to my dad was putting the squeeze on him financially. The IRS even got involved, making threatening phone calls and doing surveillance on our house. If they were watching that Christmas morning, they would have gotten an eye full. Unfortunately, the troubles never stopped, and several years later my dad was forced to sell his business.

Looking back now as an adult and father, I can better understand the pressure and stress my parents were under. The Erector set and Lincoln Logs represented the best they could do at the time. They loved us more than we could ever imagine. They were facing challenges greater than we would ever know. I am much more grateful for the Lincoln Logs today than ever before. Plus, what parent among us hasn't braved the wilds of a late-night Christmas Eve on an acquisition mission to get the perfect last-minute toy for our kids? Why do we do such crazy and unreasonable things any sane person wouldn't dare do? Why would we go where even angels fear to tread? Because we love our kids. Because we'd die trying to make a Christmas memorable and magical for them.

What were the lives of the shepherds like on that night? What was on their minds? Were they thinking about their families? Were they missing their little ones? Did a young shepherd long to get back to town the next day to get just one glimpse of his bride to be? The time of year was known for the ewes giving birth. Were some shepherds on labor and delivery duty? Did others ponder what their income would be in a few weeks when they would guide the young lambs north to Jerusalem to be sold at the Temple for sacrifices?

Whatever the thoughts might have been, the angel broke the stillness of the night. Luke mentions their fear. The angels tell the shepherds to do just the opposite.

"Don't be afraid. We've got incredible news for you. And, not just for you, but for everybody, and I mean everybody." [1]

The angel went on to explain what the news was. God was setting the stage in their backyard to bring to earth His son, the long-awaited Messiah, the promised one, who would rule the people. What did this news mean for them? No more stress and pressure of exorbitant taxes. No more dealing with the shrewdness and rudeness of the religious leaders. The Messiah meant respect and value for all people. No longer would the shepherds be treated like social outcasts just one rung away from the lepers.

The angel told the shepherds where to look. "You'll find him in the city; he'll be wrapped in rags lying in, of all places, a manger."[2]

How many babies were born that night in Bethlehem? I don't know. But, if there was more than one, Jesus would at least stand out with his swaddling strips of cloth and the feed trough filled with hay.

The angel finishes this powerful monologue, and suddenly a host of innumerable angels begins to praise God saying, "Glory to God in the highest, and on earth peace, goodwill toward men."[3] In our modern-day vernacular, it would read: "This is for God's glory and your good ... and it's really good."

With that, the angels disappear and leave the shepherds to commence their scavenger hunt for the baby born in Bethlehem.

God does this in our lives at times. He'll shake things up and sift things out. He will bring new challenges and remove familiar comforts.

Why does God interrupt us at the most inopportune times of life? Because he loves us. The news to the shepherds wasn't about them or because of them. Just like Mary and Joseph, they would have attended synagogue. As blue-collar, third shift workers, they followed a trade instead of furthering their education in the synagogue and devoting their lives to following a rabbi.

Life gets busy. Things distract us from the most important priorities. God is good and gracious enough to tap us on the shoulder and say, "Hey, I'm doing something. Pay attention." We should all know better and do better. God knows us, as the Psalmist says, that we are but dust and like the grass of the field.[4] We are fragile and fickle creatures. We need a little boost, a little nudge, and a little love pointing us in the right direction.

As you celebrate the holidays, watch for the little nudge and know it is God's little bit of love. When God has our attention, we have no telling what He can and will do in, through, and in front of our lives. Are we willing to be interrupted?

God's message to Mary: be patient. God's message to Joseph: be faithful. Now, God's message to the shepherds was: be willing.

Chapter Sixteen

A Willing Wonder

Headlights flashed around the corner of the building. The car engine roared as it sped toward us. It was an hour until midnight. Curfew was long gone. My roommate and I dove into the bushes to try and hide from campus security. "Shhh! They'll hear us if you don't stop laughing," Ryan said to me. I couldn't help myself. We were behind the dining hall hiding in the woods. West Virginia had good woods to hide in, especially at night. Gravel crunched under the tires of the college campus security vehicle, which was just the beater car owned by whichever college guy was on duty that night for security. His Maglite flashlight shined this way and that like a spotlight from a police cruiser. I couldn't help but laugh. "Shut up, man!

You're gonna get us caught." The sight of Ryan diving into the underbrush barely able to keep his basketball shorts up was just too much for me. I was in a pair of jeans and flips flops. Ryan had an undershirt and flip flops to complete his ensemble. What were we doing hiding in the woods in the cold?

It was my freshman year at Bible college in West Virginia. The dorm held a competition each year just before Christmas break. The dorm wing with the best decorations and most creative theme would win piz-za and soda. We had a week to prepare. The judging would happen on Saturday and winners would be an-nounced the following Monday night. It was Friday night, and we had nothing in the hall. The floor leader for our wing pulled a quick meeting just before curfew. We circled around in the hallway to hear what his plan was.

"Hey guys, we're kind of behind the eight ball with getting the hall decorated," Daniel said.

"Yeah, no kidding," one of the guys shouted.

"Shut your pie hole, Pierson," someone chided.

"Okay, okay, easy guys. So, here's the deal. We need to come up with a theme and then decorate the doors to our rooms and anything else we can do to dress up the hallway. I know it's late in the game, but we'll do the best we can. Any ideas?" Daniel asked.

"Santa's workshop" someone suggested.

"Nativity" added another.

"The toy department at Walmart the day after Christmas."

"What? Dude, that's stupid. What are you talking about?"

"It's empty. We just need to pull empty bookshelves and milk crates into the hallway. Some of you guys have milk crates you use for your books, right?"

"You're an idiot, Sanders," another guy pushed back.

"What about a Charlie Brown Christmas?" someone asked.

"That's a perfect idea," Daniel said.

"I've got some white snow spray we can use to write on the hall walls, or we could make big snowflakes," another guy suggested.

"Okay, everybody got the idea? Manney and LeBlanc stay after the meeting," Daniel asked.

The meeting was finished, and guys started pulling decorations out of their rooms. Garland, strings of lights, and cheap red bows from the dollar store began to bring life to our institutional cinder block, two-toned hallway. Someone started spraying "Merry Christmas" with the can of snow spray. The walls were painted blue from the floor halfway up the wall and transitioned to white at the four-foot point. I looked at the "Merry Christmas" on the section of blue paint. *I don't think this is going to come off,* I thought.

Daniel caught me mid-thought. "Hey, Matt. Can you and Ryan work on getting us a tree?" he asked. "Like a Christmas tree?" Ryan asked. "Yeah, just run up the hill and cut one down in the woods," Daniel said. "Us and what chainsaw?" Ryan shot back. "We'll figure it out. Come on, man. Let's go," I said as I grabbed Ryan around the shoulder. "Are we good to go out even though it's after curfew?" I called over my shoulder to Daniel. "Yeah, just be quick. It shouldn't take more than five minutes," he said.

Twenty minutes later, Ryan and I were hiding in the woods on the other side of campus. Who was Daniel kidding? We weren't going to magically find a fresh-cut pine tree. Here we were looking at getting written up for being out past curfew.

We were crouched behind some bushes when the light of the flashlight landed on two pairs of bare feet in flip-flops and then traveled up to our faces.

"Hey, what in the world are you guys doing?" the security guy shouted to us as he got out of his car.

We stood up. Caught red-handed. "Uh, were just out looking for pine branches and stuff to decorate the dorm for Christmas," I said.

"You guys aren't supposed to be out here after curfew. And why are you both in t-shirts?" he asked.

We just smiled and shrugged our shoulders.

"Listen, get back to your dorm or else I'm going to write you up," he said.

"No problem, man. We're heading back right now," Ryan said.

The security guy got back in his car, started the engine, and pulled away.

"What are you doing?" Ryan asked as he turned around to look at me. I was pulling on a small pine tree that was scrawny. "I'm trying to get us a tree," I said.

"That's not a tree. That's a pine branch," he said.

"Dude, Charlie Brown's tree looked horrible, too.

It'll be fine," I argued.

We took the poor excuse for a pine tree back to the dorm. I cobbled together an angel for the top from an empty paper towel roll and some creative license with coffee filters.

We took first place for the dorm decoration competition. The pizza party was perfect, and the snow spray didn't come off the wall. We had to scrub down all the walls before we could go home for winter break. Lesson learned.

———————

The shepherds were on the hunt, as well, the night they had the close encounter. They weren't looking for a would-be tree. They were looking for a baby.

What would set Jesus apart from any other baby potentially born that night was the location and identification. The location was a stable. This was not the normal place you'd put a baby. Just in case other babies were being born in stables, the other indication was that he'd be the baby wrapped in swaddling clothes.

Why indicate swaddling clothes?

Some scholars believe the shepherds weren't just any run-of-the-mill shepherds. They believe they were Levitical shepherds who were specially trained and handpicked to watch over the flocks of sheep used for sacrifice in the temple. One of the major responsibilities was to keep the sheep safe and from getting dirty. To keep the young lambs clean and protected, the shepherds used a technique in which they would wrap the lambs in strips of cloth. This technique was called "swaddling." Some even go so far as to believe the cloth was from worn-out robes of temple priests. Instead of discarding the sacred robes, they would cut them into strips to be reused in the swaddling process. You can begin to connect the dots and see the imagery of little lambs being swaddled and a baby being swaddled. That baby would one day be called the Lamb of God, fulfilling this title by "taking away the sin of the world."[1]

If you stop and pause for a moment, you can begin to find there is so much more to celebrate than chocolate Santas and stockings hung by the chimney with care. Are you willing to look for more in the manger? Could there be more to the story than just a "what we see is what we get" mindset?

A willing heart and a wondering mind can be far more engaged with God than going through the motions of the holidays. Maybe what you've always been looking for can be found in the manger, if you're willing.

Chapter Seventeen

Christmas in Perspective

"Dad, Dad … the trash man took our car!" Malachi shouted.

The trash man took our car? I thought. "What are you talking about, Bud?" I asked.

"Maggie's red car. It's gone," he said.

"Oh, boy," I said.

It was Monday, just a week before Christmas. Each of the kids had a set of wheels to cruise up and down our one-way street. Malachi and Madison had bicycles. Maggie had a Little Tikes Cozy Coupe, the one with a yellow hardtop and red body. The whole month of December they were outside as much as possible watching the neighborhood transform before their eyes into a winter wonderland. Birchwood Road was the block to drive if you were looking for some good Christmas displays.

The problem began the Saturday before that infamous Monday. We did our part earlier Saturday morning and pulled our decorations from the basement. A yard inflatable of a Dalmatian dressed in a fireman's hat with a present sitting in between his paws sat on one side of the yard. We set up a snowman and another inflatable dog on the other side of the lawn. That dog was dressed up as a police dog. Both dog inflatables were from one of our kid's favorite television shows. I untangled a bundle of multicolored lights and strung them across the top of our three-foot-high green chain-link fence. Amanda stood on a step ladder and strung icicle light across the front of the house along the gutters. The kids scooted up and down the street reporting what the other neighbors were adding to their displays.

"Dad, Miss Bobbi and Mr. Bernie have a baby Jesus out," Maddie announced.

"Mr. Phil and Miss Lynn have giant candy canes along their driveway," Malachi shouted from the other end of the block. Maggie scooted up and down the street in her Cozy Coupe.

I pulled out a few sets of net lights to drape over the large rhododendron bush at the corner of the house and then a few on a holly bush by the front step. Amanda finished up with the icicle lights.

"All right, guys, it's almost dark out. Let's plug everything in and see what happens. Are you ready?" I asked. The kids cheered. I found the timer that controlled all the lights and inflatables in the yard. A tangled network of white, brown, orange, and green extension cords snaked their way from all corners of the yard to my little timer by the front step.

"Here we go. Count it down with me," I said.

"Five, four, three, two, one!" we shouted.

I flipped the switch. Inflatables started blowing up and coming to life. I looked at my handiwork on the fence line. The colored lights looked great except for a strand of lights that was dark. The icicle light looked great until a strand became unhooked from the gutter and swagged across our front window. The police dog looked good. The fireman dog was face down on the ground with its backside pointing to the sky. The snowman was fully inflated. The only problem was that his little light inside was dark.

"Hey Dad, why isn't some of the stuff working?" the kids asked.

I was flustered. "I don't know. Let's go inside and regroup with some dinner," I said.

"And don't forget to put your bikes and car next to the side of the house," I added.

The next morning, I saw Maggie's car sitting outside our front gate on the two-foot patch of grass between the sidewalk and the roadway.

"Mags, sweetheart, don't forget to put your car by the house," I told her as we loaded up in the van to go to the church.

We came home that afternoon, had lunch, and the kids played outside again, giving reports of the continued progress of each home. Amanda and I tackled the lights that weren't cooperating. By dusk, everything was operational. We stood out on the street and looked at the front of the house. Finally, our place was decorated. As I walked back to the house, I saw Maggie's Cozy Coupe parked by the road again.

"Hey, baby, you need to put your car by the house," I told her.

"Okay, Daddy, I'll get it." She ran off toward the

house.

The car sat by the road. A good dad would have just grabbed the car and set it by the house. I wasn't a good dad that night. I wasn't in the mood to deal with a Cozy Coupe. I wanted to get into my cozy home for the night and go to bed.

Monday came and the kids were playing outside again. Amanda was baking some chocolate chip cookies. It was my day off, so I was busy binge-watching a Netflix series. In my subconscious, I heard the rumbling of the trash truck.

Oh, man. Did I remember to put the trash out? I thought. *I did. I put it out just before we came in the house last night*, I remembered.

Then it happened: "Dad, Dad ..."

You know the rest.

"Guys, why didn't you grab Maggie's car?" I asked.

"Well, we saw the truck coming and then the trash man just grabbed the car and tossed it into the back of the trash truck," Malachi explained.

"Where was the car?" I asked.

"It was right by the road," Madison said.

"Mags ..."

"Yes, Daddy?" she said.

"Honey, why didn't you pull your car into the yard after you were done playing?"

My little blondie just shrugged and smiled at me.

She knows my weak spot. How was I going to be upset with my little girl? But, now, I had a bigger problem. How was I going to replace that car by Christmas?

———————

The shepherds have much to teach us about being willing amid the wonder of Christmas. They have a lot to teach a dad who's about to go looking for a last-minute gift for his towheaded toddler.

1. Look for the God moments, not just the good moments.

We can become so fixated on the perfect Christmas that we miss the present Christmas. What do I mean by "present Christmas"? We work to a preferred vision of what we think our lives should look like; we miss the opportunity to learn from the present. Any time life takes a hard right, throws you into a tailspin, or ends up in a head-on collision, you can be sure to look for God in the moment. Does God cause chaos, pain, loss, interruption, irritation, or frustration? No, but we can look for the choice to acknowledge God amid the chaos. We can choose to reflect Jesus to the people watching. Did my little girl need a lecture? Maybe. More than anything, she needed a daddy who was going to see through the irritation. Should she have pulled the car in? Sure. Should I have pulled the car in by the house? Probably. In the end, we couldn't go back and change any of that. Yelling at her wouldn't fix anything. Sometimes stressful events unfold, accidents happen, and life is, well, just that—life.

Our goal is to look for God. How can we find God in the midst of this?

2. Keep your work in perspective.

For the shepherds, the interruption cut into their routine, their sleep, and caring for the sheep. Sometimes interruptions happen to help us keep perspective. This interruption was going to take precedence over anyone trying to get a tight eight hours of sleep. Any tiredness they would experience the next day was well worth it.

The job, the project, and the promotion all compete for our attention. While they occupy us, they cannot define us. There will be times we need to take a break, cut loose, and shut it off until tomorrow. The work will be there the next day, and the next, and the day after that. Our kids, friends, and opportunities to connect and be a part of God's work may not be there the next day.

3. Don't underestimate a fearful situation.

God's plan to do something great initially created fear for the shepherds. God may be inviting you to do something that initially creates fear within. Don't miss what God is doing because fear has paralyzed you.

The encouragement from the angels to the shepherds was "Don't be afraid." The alternative response the angelic host offered was "But celebrate!" How can we turn fear into joy? The angel said the event happening down in Bethlehem was going to be good news and bring great joy to all people.

What was the good news? Jesus was going to make it possible for us to connect to God once again, like Adam and Eve had in the Garden of Eden. If we could have a relationship with God, it would have ramifications beyond our vertical connection with God. It would also mean the ability to have better relationships with those around us.

———————

Shepherds left their flocks for a moment and went into the city to find Jesus. It was in the interruption of that moment that God was making something truly wonderful known to the shepherds. God can reveal himself in and through the interruptions of life. We need to be willing to look for God in the interruptions.

Chapter Eighteen

Christmas Invitation

The Cozy Coupe episode shouldn't have been a big deal, but I couldn't let it go. I felt bad. I wanted Christmas to be special for Maggie. Christmas was only a few days away. I looked online to see if I could order a replacement car for her and get it in time to put it under the tree for Christmas morning. That option was a no go. It was impossible to get it in time. I searched online to see if any big box stores had any Cozy Coupes in stock. Again, no go.

Christmas Eve day came, and I was determined to find this stupid car. Yes, it had now come to that. It had officially gone to "stupid" level status.

I had one last place to look, the local Babies "R" Us. The Cozy Coupe wasn't a baby thing, but I figured I'd give it a shot. I found one listed in stock on their website, and the store just so happened to be on the way to church. We had a Christmas Eve service, so I figured I would stop by on my way to the service and get the car. At the time, we had two vans, so this worked out great. Amanda and the kids would go to church in the nice van. I'd take the beater van to Babies "R" Us and snag the last car in stock. I called the store beforehand just to be sure they still had it. The store associate assured me it was in stock, but they couldn't hold it for me.

I had a dilemma. The store wouldn't be open when we got done with the Christmas Eve service, so I would have to hustle and stop by on my way to church.

It seemed like I hit every red light on the way to the store. *What in the world?!* I thought. *I can't be late to church, and I've got to get this car before the store closes.* I was stressed.

I pulled into the parking spot with a screech of the tires, threw the gear selector into PARK, and hopped out of the van. The doors to the store seemed to slide open as slowly as possible. Perspiration was forming on my forehead. I had the appearance of a wild game hunter looking for his prey. I started speed walking past each aisle until I found the "Bouncers/Riders" section.

"Hey, Pastor Matt," I heard from behind me. *Oh, man, not now. Who could this be?* It was Christmas Eve. I'm a pastor. And somebody has it planned to hijack my attention at the worst possible time.

I turned and saw a guy who had attended our church on and off for a while.

"Hey, John. How are you?" I asked.

"Good. How are you?"

"I'm good. Are you doing some last-minute Christmas shopping?" I asked as I turned to look back down the aisle to see if I could spy the classic red and yellow car.

"I am. And, by the looks of it, so are you. What are you looking for?" he asked.

I don't have the time for this. This guy hasn't been to church in forever. He's not coming to the Christmas Eve service. The last time we talked, he told me he thought a cataclysmic event was going to happen before Christmas. It didn't. Otherwise, none of us would be here. I bet he's gonna ask me about that. I don't have time to get into a discussion about ...

"Hey, so what are you looking for?" he asked again as he broke my train of thought.

"Um, I'm looking for one of those little yellow and red cars that toddlers like to scoot around in, but I can't find it."

I can't believe this. Not only am I not finding the car. Now I'm stuck talking. To top it all off, I'm going to be late to church, I thought.

"Um, well, I think I see one right there," he pointed.

"Where?" I asked.

He walked past me and stood right in front of a single box sitting on a middle shelf.

"Right here," he said. "It's not yellow and red, but it's pink. Does that work?" he asked.

Relief swept over me.

"Yeah, that's perfect," I said with a smile. "Thanks, John. I really appreciate it!"

"Merry Christmas," he said.

"Merry Christmas, John. Thanks for the help," I said.

My heart was humbled. I looked at my watch. *If I can pay for this quick and hit some green lights, I should make it to church on time,* I thought.

140

I got out to the van and opened the back hatch. What I saw sitting in the rear storage compartment made my heart drop.

Oh, man. I completely forgot, I thought. I pulled the oversized pink Cozy Coupe box from the shopping cart and tucked it in the back of the van.

I'd have to figure out what to do with what was in the back of the van. For now, I had to get to church.

———————

Before we can leave the shepherds and move on to one of the more infamous characters of the Christmas story, Herod, we have a few final thoughts about the part they play in welcoming Jesus to our world.

1. Interruptions take us from hearing and knowing to seeing and believing.

The anticipation of the shepherds turned into a realization for the shepherds. What's interesting is that, as the rest of the story unfolds, you won't find the religious leaders of the Jews in their expensive robes and formal hats coming to make an audience before the newborn king. They knew the signs. They had the information, but never got an invitation.

How often do we miss out on seeing God doing something in our lives because we settle for information in place of an invitation? Interruptions are God's invitation to see him work. Life can become so fast-paced we miss these moments. We find ourselves getting so busy and hustling so much, we don't even realize we are competing against a figment of something illusionary. Jon Acuff describes it this way: "[We] feel the need to "get ahead." In those moments, it's helpful for me to stop for a second and ask, "Get ahead of what?" The answer is often the expectations of others or my secret, unreasonable expectations. Chasing either is no fun."[1]

I love the truth of his statement. I find, it's when we stop "chasing" that we go from hearing about God working to believing and seeing God working.

2. Interruptions won't make sense to everyone.

When the shepherds came to the stable, they couldn't contain themselves. The left the manger amazed. They were so compelled by what they had seen that they told anyone and everyone they saw about it.

The people they saw responded not as we might have hoped. Luke tells us, "All who heard wondered about the things the shepherds had told them."[2] He doesn't say, "And they followed up on what they heard to confirm the news from the shepherds." The people responded with, "Huh, that's interesting. Now, Martha, pass the gravy." They continued with life as if nothing had happened worth stopping for.

The moments God begins to work in your life and around your life not everyone will get it. That's okay. You do you. You follow the leading. Trace the gingerbread crumbs and the magical little interruptions, because they will lead you to a manger. They will lead you to a moment that will change how you view life. These moments have the power to change you if you will let them.

———————

"Dad, can we? Can we, please?" my kids asked after the Christmas Eve service.

"Let me talk to your mom first and we'll figure it out," I said.

Our usual tradition was to stop at the local McDonald's and grab a couple of hot chocolates and then drive around the neighborhoods and look at the Christmas displays and lights people had decorated their homes with.

"What do you think, babe? Did you get the car okay?" Amanda whispered to me.

"We're all good. I picked it up with no problem. I'm good to do lights if you're okay with it. Let's go home first and regroup. I'll park the van and then hop in with you and the kids. We can swing by McDonald's and grab hot chocolates, then look at lights."

I climbed into the van and looked through the passenger window as Amanda strapped in the last kiddo. She climbed into the driver's seat of her van and looked at me. I smiled and gave her a thumbs-up. She smiled back and waved.

I put the van in reverse and looked in my rearview mirror to back out. I saw the Cozy Coupe angled awkwardly in the back.

That's right. I forgot, I remembered. Then my internal dialogue kicked into high gear.

In the first week of December, I received a call from

a single mom who found our information online.

"Hi, Pastor Manney," she said when I answered her call. "I was just calling to see if you guys helped out families for Christmas?" she asked.

I got some of her story and what they were facing as a family. She had two boys, one in high school and the other in middle school, as well as a little girl in pre-school.

I asked her what they needed and told her I would ask our church to donate items and gifts to help her family out at Christmas.

"We'd be happy to help. I'll be sure to drop off a box to you before Christmas," I told her.

Fast-forward to Christmas Eve. That box of gifts and donations was sitting in the back of my van next to a pink Cozy Coupe.

What should I do? I haven't heard from her again. I don't even know if the call was legit. Maybe it was a scam. That's happened before. What if I just dropped it off on Christmas Day? Nah, I don't want to do that. Maybe tonight? I can't do that because Amanda and the kids are waiting for me. But I went through all that trouble to get my little girl her Christmas present. Shouldn't I make sure a family has their

Christmas presents, too? If Maggie wouldn't have left her car by the road, then I wouldn't have gone to Babies "R" Us, and then I would have never seen the ... Oh, I get it now, I thought. I started to connect the dots, and it became crystal clear what I needed to do.

I pulled up the lady's information on my phone and punched the address into my map application. Her home was on the way to the house. *I'll make it quick,* I thought.

I pulled up to the house. It was a rowhome tucked in with a few homes on either side and a small fenced-in yard. It was dark—no Christmas lights, no yard inflatables, no Cozy Coupe. Just a few broken toys were strewn about the yard. A few pairs of worn-out kids' boots were set by the front steps. I opened the back hatch and pulled the box of Christmas presents from the van. The front gate opened with a squeak. *Needs some WD-40.*

It didn't look like anyone was home, but I saw a blue hue and shifting shadows through the window curtains, as if a television was on.

I may as well give it a try.

I knocked on the door and stepped back. I didn't

want to frighten anyone who would be answering the door.

No answer. I knocked again.

The drapes pulled back slightly, and I saw a shadow. I smiled and waved to put them at ease.

The door opened and a young middle school-aged boy pushed the screen door open.

"Hey, bud. My name is Matt. I'm the pastor of a church across town."

He didn't say anything.

"Your mom called and asked if we could help with Christmas. I've got a box of gifts for you and your family."

He just looked at me.

"Do you mind if I drop this off with you? It's kind of a big box. I can carry it in if you like?" I asked.

He pushed the door open wider and let me in.

The living room was dark except for the television and a small artificial tree sitting in the corner. The tree had one string of lights and a few ornaments.

"There's some stuff in here for your mom and sister. There are a few gifts for you and your older brother, too. Better open them up before he gets to them so you can get the good gifts," I teased him.

He laughed and said, "Thanks."

"All right, man. Tell your mom I said 'hi' and, um …"

"My mom is out with my brother and sister," he cut in.

It was the first time he had said more than one word. I'd be a little cautious, too, if a big guy with a suit and tie on came to my front door on Christmas Eve. Santa's hired the Mafia to deliver gifts this year—or the IRS.

"Okay, great. Well, tell them I said, 'Merry Christmas,'" I said as I pushed open the door.

"Okay, thanks. You, too," he said as he stood at the door and waved to me. I waved back as I walked back down the sidewalk to my van.

Man, that must be a tough Christmas for them. No presents under the tree on Christmas Eve. Barely a Christmas tree, at that. I feel bad I almost didn't make it a point to stop by tonight. But I'm really glad I did, I thought.

I got back in the van, buckled up, and pulled out my cell.

"Hey, babe, just dropped off that Christmas box," I texted.

"Oh, great! Thanks for doing that," she replied.

"Ready for some lights and hot chocolate. It's going to be a good night!" I texted.

"Definitely!" she texted back.

I pulled away from the house as one last thought crossed my mind: *I hope I had the right house and address for the family. Otherwise, that kid just made out like a bandit.*

I double-checked the address on my phone. Right address. Right interruption. Best invitation from God.

Chapter Nineteen

Chaos of Christmas

Meanwhile, in a city on another hillside, a king paced and plotted. This is the slightly darker side of the Christmas story.

In church Christmas plays, if this character is even included in the play, the play director often typecasts the infamous King Herod as the angry third-grade bully. Who can you trust to lose his temper on cue? The kid in the red t-shirt. At least he's usually wearing red.

In every story, if it's going to be a good story, you need a villain. Herod is the villain in our Christmas story. The nice part of all this is that even villains have something to teach us.

History leaves us nothing truly good to know about Herod. He was the one who built the great Temple in

Jerusalem, and that's about it. If he was going to be written up in Santa's book of naughty and nice kids, he'd be on the naughty list ... probably at the top.

Herod's wealth is estimated by some scholars to have been one hundred times that of the gross domestic product of the entire country of Israel.[1] He built lavish palaces throughout his kingdom. Backed by the Roman Republic, he was crowned "King of the Jews," which the Jews themselves didn't like. Herod was an Edomite by ethnicity. Here's a little history between the Jews and the Edomites.

Numbers 24:17 describes a scepter rising out of Jacob and overthrowing Edom. This was a prophecy on the hearts and minds of the Jews. Jacob was a twin. His older brother, by a few minutes, was Esau. If you remember your Sunday school lesson, Jacob conned Esau out of his birthright and blessing from their father Isaac. For centuries, there was bad blood between the Jews and their cousins the Edomites, the descendants of Esau. Herod, an Edomite ruling the Jews, was just more salt being pressed into the wound.

Some Jews figured that, if they couldn't fight Herod, they should join him, so they created a cult following of Herod. They were called Herodians and sought to create a theocracy claiming Herod as Jehovah's promised Messiah. You can see how this is politically shaping the landscape into which Jesus was born.

Herod was a paranoid megalomaniac. He had his wife, the two sons they shared, his mother-in-law, and his wife's grandfather all killed. He was so ruthless to the people he ruled over that he ordered the execution of popular public leaders so that the people, while they would not mourn his death, would be mourning the death of their loved ones the day Herod died.

So, this is the man ruling and reigning the world Jesus was about to be born into. A man so powerful, so angry, and so paranoid that he would miss the most incredible event in all of history. Instead of celebrating, he would be fighting a conflict he would never win.

———————

Christmas can be a tough time for some people. It can be a time filled with worry and sadness. Some experts have coined the phrase seasonal affective disorder (SAD) to describe the anxiety and depression people suffer from during this time. Why? The depression may come because of the loss of a loved one. This will be the first Christmas with their loved one's chair sitting empty at the dinner table. Others may have experienced the loss of a job. The boss couldn't afford to keep them through the holidays, so they got a layoff notice. Then there are the macro problems facing our society today: terrorism, gun violence, abortion, domestic abuse, financial crisis, and mental health issues. We live in the tension of hope and hurt. We hurt because of the reality of the lives we live. We hope for relief to come, for the wrong in our world to be made right. We long for a day when we will no longer fear.

Christmas strikes at the heart of this tension within us. The tension experienced by the people whose lives and stories intersect the Christmas story is no different. While we find ourselves enraptured by the story of the manger, we shy away from the cruelty of the king in residence in his palace only a few miles away. The closer we look and deepen our understanding of the tension Joseph and Mary faced, the more we will begin to understand how their story impacts our story. The hope they had under the tyranny of Herod's cruel hand can be the same hope we hold on to in the difficult situations we face. Hope can turn the chaos into calm when we look for the rays of hope within our story.

Chapter Twenty

Joy of a Moment

Celebrating Christmas is the highlight of my year. But, I'll confess, sometimes I'm not in the mood. I've got a friend, and I'm sure you've got one of those friends, too: they don't like Christmas. They don't like the lights, the music, and especially giving gifts. They've got a little bit of the Grinch and Ebenezer Scrooge in them. Don't we all, though, if left unchecked? I'm hard on my buddy, but I get it. I get overwhelmed by the holidays, and if I'm not careful, that "overwhelm" can turn into a critical spirit, then resentment, and that resentment can transform into bitterness.

So, what do I do to get out of a bad headspace? I remember some of my best Christmas memories.

Do you remember my trip to Victoria Garden with

Amanda and the ring in my pocket? Let's pick up from there.

Fast forward to just a few weeks after that trip to the beautiful winter wonderland at the mall. We were planning for Christmas break, a couple of weeks away from the strain of juggling college classes, ministry in Mojave, and working security at the aerospace company down the road from the college. I was hoping to visit Amanda and her family in Illinois for a few days. Most of all, I was hoping to have Amanda meet my family for the first time and maybe pop the question.

Just before we went our separate ways for winter break, we talked about our future.

"So, what do you think about a winter wedding?" I asked.

"Yeah, I guess so. I guess that would be fun to decorate the church with a winterish theme," Amanda said.

"So ... what are your thoughts about getting engaged?" I asked. I'm sly about this kind of stuff. I was trying to nail down when I could ask her to marry me.

"I don't want to be engaged for more than a year, I think. So, maybe next fall or Christmas?" she thought.

"What do you think about getting married next

Christmas?" I suggested.

"You mean, like, right after I finish with school?" she asked.

"I guess I could make that work. But what about you? What about a job, a place to live? And I've only met your parents once. Are you sure they like me?" she asked.

"I don't think that's going to be an issue. My parents love you, and I met your family this past summer, and I love them. I think they like me, right?"

"Yeah, babe, you're good," she said with a smile.

"Let's keep talking about it. I want to get through the holidays; then we'll go from there. Is that okay?" she asked.

"Yeah, that'll be okay," I said with a grin. She was giving me a yellow light. What do you do at a yellow light? You hit the gas pedal.

————

The flight from Los Angeles to Philadelphia seemed like a flash. I couldn't stop thinking about the ring, our plans, and getting married. I turned on the inflight movie selections to get my mind off things and saw that a new Christmas movie called *Elf* was available to watch. My Christmas movie must-watch list just blew up. Every Christmas movie I thought I loved just got knocked down a peg. The movie was all things Christmas, not to mention the love story and humor. Who doesn't love a good romantic comedy about an elf? I began planning in my mind for when Amanda came in just a few days: we would drive up to New York City, take a carriage ride to the huge Christmas tree in front of Rockefeller Center, and then I would get down on one knee. It was going to be perfect.

Amanda flew in on a Monday morning. I was planning to make the trip to New York on Tuesday morning. Late Monday night, the news reported: "NYC public transportation is going on strike. If you're planning to come to New York on Tuesday, don't."

What do they mean 'don't'? I thought. I was scrambling to figure out what to do. I made a call to my brother.

"Hey, Matt, what's up?" he answered.

"Mike, I'm in a jam. I'm supposed to go to New York tomorrow and propose to Amanda, but New York City public transit is going on strike. They said don't even bother coming to New York. What am I going to do?" I panicked.

"What about Philly?" he asked.

"Yeah, I guess so. I just don't even know where to go," I said.

"I'll talk to Melissa and we'll think of something. Don't worry. It'll all work out," he reassured me.

The next day, I told Amanda there was a change of plans, and we'd be heading to Philadelphia instead of New York. We left for Philly late in the afternoon. When I say we, I mean my entire family: my parents, my sister Sarah, Mike and his wife Melissa, and the neighbor's dog. No dog, but you get the idea. With the whole family going, Amanda would have no idea what was coming.

The first stop was at a little Italian bakery in the heart of Philly. We piled into the tiny storefront. You could smell cookies baking and coffee brewing, and hear Christmas music playing softly in the background. Amanda and I shared a cup of hot chocolate and cannoli. We laughed and talked about what our next stop would be.

What would the next stop be? I thought. I whispered to Mike on the way out of the bakery, "Where to next?"

"Well, what are you thinking?" he asked me.

"I'm kinda nervous and I want to just bite the bullet and ask her. I'm thinking the carriage ride at Independence Hall," I said.

"Great, well go there next," he said.

My parents and sister got in their car, and Amanda and I rode with Mike and Melissa in their SUV.

We pulled up to Independence Hall and looked for where the horse and carriage rides were usually set up. No horses. No carriages. We asked a policeman walking past us where the carriage rides were. He said it was too cold for the carriage rides.

Oh man, this is not happening!

I shot a text to Mike's phone: "Where are you thinking to take us?" Melissa responded on his phone while he drove.

"Love Park," it said, with a smiley face.

Love Park was a great spot with an art piece that had the letters L-O-V-E spelled out with the L and O on top of the V and E.

"Perfect," I texted back. I didn't care where it was, I

just needed a place to kneel and open a ring box.

We pulled up to the park, and none of the park lights were on. No Christmas lights were adorning the trees or bushes. A homeless guy was sleeping on a park bench, and another was pushing a shopping cart loaded down with bags past us while eyeing the SUV.

"You know, maybe we should try this another time," Mike said.

I don't think I'm supposed to get engaged today. Maybe God doesn't want this to happen.

"We've got one more place to try. Don't worry. We've got this," Melissa texted to my phone.

A few minutes later, we pulled into the parking lot across from the Philadelphia Museum of Art, made famous as the steps Sylvester Stallone (Rocky Balboa) ran up in the movie *Rocky*. In the spring and summer, there is a beautiful water fountain. For the holidays, they place a thirty-foot Christmas tree decorated with ornaments and lights in the center of the now-empty fountain.

We started getting out of the SUV.

"Hey, why don't you guys go on ahead of us. We'll catch up in a minute," Mike said to Amanda and me.

"Should we wait for your family?" she asked me.

"Nah, they're good," I said.

"Are you sure?" she asked again.

I put my arm around her and pulled her close. "We're good. They'll catch up," I said with a smile.

We walked across the street and began to ascend the steps. As soon as we reached the top, the Christmas tree sparkled and glistened in the cold winter night. We turned to look at Philadelphia and the city was twinkling, with light scattered across the skyline. It was so beautiful. *Mike and Melissa made such a good call,* I thought while I held the ring box in my jacket pocket.

I looked at Amanda. Her nose was red from the cold.

"This is beautiful, but I'm getting cold. Do you want to wait for your family or go back down to the car?" she asked.

"Um, you know how I've been acting funny the last few days?" I said.

"Yeah," she said, as her lips quivered and breath dissipated in the cold air.

"I've been wanting to ask you something," I said.

She was still looking out at the city with her arms folded, trying to stay warm, but then turned toward me.

I got down on one knee and said, "Well, I wanted to know if you would marry me."

She was surprised and asked, "Are you serious? Do you have a ring?"

I was so nervous I had forgotten to pull the ring up and give it to her.

I pulled the ring from my jacket pocket and opened the box. The diamonds caught the faint light from the Christmas tree and sparkled.

"Well, what do you think?" I asked.

"Yes," she whispered.

I stood up and put the ring on her finger and then wrapped my arms around her and kissed her. By this point, the rest of the crew was at the bottom of the steps. I heard a whistle and cheer from my brother. They all joined us at the top of the steps and took pictures. We made quick work of the pictures and finished off the night with dinner at the Spaghetti Warehouse. Amanda and I sat at our own table while my family sat across the way. They were just close enough we could all talk and laugh, but far enough we could say sweet nothings to each other and enjoy the moment. We laughed and talked while the classic Andy Williams song played, "It's the Most Wonderful Time of the Year." As I held Amanda's hand, I thought, *This is the most wonderful time of the year.*

It's when I lose sight of all God has given me that I call to mind moments like that. Those memories help to put life in perspective. Life is about love and relationships. Life is more than what you have. Life is about who you have. Herod missed this.

Chapter Twenty-One

Humbug Holidays

"Hey, it's starting!" Commercials had been airing for weeks leading up to the big show. The words Will Vinton's *Claymation Christmas Celebration* came on the television. My favorite thing at that age in 1987 was the California Raisins. My very first backpack for school was a California Raisins backpack. As my family gathered around the glow of the TV, I was lost in the wonder of the claymation stop-motion animation. I couldn't wait to watch this Christmas special.

You can search for the special on YouTube and still watch clips of it today over thirty years later. The animation has lost a little quality compared with today's standard fare animation, but the nostalgia brings back so many great memories.

Each Christmas, I pull out DVDs of the Christmas special *Rudolf the Red-Nosed Reindeer*, another stop-motion animation. I attempt to show my kids what Daddy used to watch when he was a kid at Christmas. But they're not having it. "Dad, this is so weird. Why do the characters look so creepy?" they ask.

Aw, well maybe another year they'll learn to appreciate true classic Christmas movies.

With the claymation special, I look back and realize the memory is better than the actual special itself. I've made more of it in my mind than it was in actuality. *Rudolf,* however, is classic and never going to go out of style. At least that's what I tell my kids.

———

Just as we can tend to exaggerate memories, I wonder if Herod realized how he was exaggerating his irrational response to the news he was about to hear.

Luke picks up the story as a hand-off from Matthew and gives more detail of the next steps of Mary and Joseph. According to Luke, Caesar August called for a census (read: taxation) across all the occupied territories of the Roman Empire (read: *The Empire Strikes Back*).

Mary comes back home to Nazareth to meet up with Joseph. No sooner is she home than Joseph tells her they need to pack and prepare for the ninety-mile journey from Nazareth to Bethlehem. Imagine being nine-months pregnant and having to make a weeklong journey. The terrain, the mode of transportation—a donkey, maybe—the pregnancy, and the timing of God's plan for Jesus to be born in Bethlehem were all coming together in this choreographed saga. Herod was missing it all.

Herod was so focused on what he wanted that he completely missed out on what he had. His paranoia got the best of him. His pride blinded him from seeing the miracle for what it was, happening under his very reign as king in Israel.

The Herodion was the third-largest palace of its day. You can imagine the wealth and power Herod possessed to pull off this immense architectural feat. The palace occupied forty-five acres of land with its surrounding buildings and structures comprising a total of two hundred acres. Threats to Herod's thrown paralyzed him to the point that he worried Cleopatra would try to invade and overthrow him. Herodion was a part of several palace fortresses he built along an escape route toward his homeland of Moab.[1]

The circular palace stood ninety feet in the air with four towers skyrocketing above the double reinforced palace walls. The royal family would occupy the rooms in these towers, as they would not only catch the cool breeze coming off the Mediterranean Sea but also provide the first view of any attacking parties coming their way.

The center courtyard had a magnificent garden, lavish baths, and a reception hall for people to gather. As if one palace wasn't enough, Herod had a lower palace built with more exotic gardens and a pool. If a baby was to be born the future king of the Jews, this would seem to be the perfect place to bring him into the world.

In one of the most overlooked acts of irony in all the Christmas story, the palace of Herod overshadowed several smaller towns down in the valley, one of which was Bethlehem. Only three miles away in the Herodi-on, Herod could have easily looked out his window on a cool, clear night and looked upon the little bustling burg of Bethlehem as its citizens prepared for the census. He could have seen people traveling from all different places converging on their hometown.[2]

There were two reasons Herod missed the most incredible moment of history:

He was distracted by his pride and paranoia.

He didn't see the value in the valley below.

How often do we exaggerate in our minds the worries and anxieties of the holiday season? We ponder and wonder things like, "Will there be enough presents for Christmas? Did I sign up for cookies or brownies for the school Christmas party? Is the Christmas Eve service at 5:30 or 7:30? Oh, right, it's both, but which one should we go to? Whose house should we go to this year? We did my parents last year, but we just had the falling out with his parents. So, should we just go back to my parents, or should we just skip going to see family all together?" There are lots of things to consider, and no way of getting around them without making decisions—and sometimes not without letting someone down.

The choices can become so overwhelming that we get to the point we don't even like celebrating Christmas because of all the expectations and pressures. We find ourselves seeing Christmas as something to be endured rather than enjoyed.

Don't get me wrong. I'm not saying we're like Herod, about to burn down the Christmas tree and throw all our kids presents away because their behavior deserves coal instead, even though we might feel like it. The question for us to consider is this: what mindset is keeping me from enjoying Christmas?

When we know the answer to that question, we can begin to make changes and slow life down. Only when we can begin to process the present are we able to enjoy the special moments and treasure the memories we are creating with the people we love the most.

Herod is not the guy we want to be like. Pride makes us miss out on the most important moments. Humility keeps our pride in check. Humility says, "I can't do it all. I can't be it all. But I will do what I can, when I can, the best I can." Then leave the rest to God. He cares more about your kids, your friendships, and your circumstances than you can imagine. Give God space to work and create a Christmas you'll never forget.

Chapter Twenty-Two

Making Memories

Picking a Christmas tree takes skill, especially if it's already bound up. Early on in our marriage, we bought a live tree every year until we didn't. When I say until we didn't, I mean I didn't want to have to deal with the hassle anymore.

As a kid, every Christmas my parents would load us up in the family wagon, and we would go shopping for a tree. One year, we drove out of town to a Christmas tree farm. The plan was to make a trek out into a field of evergreens and chop down our very own tree. It sounds fantastic, wonderful, and the stuff memories are made of. It was wonderful, with the exception that we didn't have an ax or saw to chop the tree down. I remember my dad hiking back up the hill to the little shed where you paid for your tree. He asked the guy managing the tree farm if he could borrow a hand saw, then came back and got to work. Cutting down the tree was more like *National Lampoon's Christmas Vacation*. My dad sawed on the tree for a while. My brother jumped in. Then I took a turn. I remember thinking, *This isn't fun anymore*. That was the last year we cut down a tree.

Fast-forward twenty years later, and Amanda and I are standing in the outdoor garden center of Lowe's. "Are you sure you want to get a real tree?" she asked me.

"Yeah, babe. We did this every year as a family tradition. It'll be fun," I said.

"What did you do as a family?" I asked.

"My dad would put up an artificial tree. He'd pull it up from the basement and then decorate it with a different theme every year," she said.

"Well, my family would buy a live tree and then we'd decorate with the same ornaments every year. You know, like homemade ornaments. One Christmas, Mike and I put the tree up ourselves. We set the tree in the corner of the family room. There were, like, four or five boxes of ornaments, and we loaded up the front of the tree. There were so many ornaments on the tree it was top-heavy and fell over just when we put the last few ornaments on the tree," I said with a laugh.

She wasn't amused. She was cold. I was trying to relive my childhood, and the kid at the cash register wanted to go home for the night because it was almost closing time.

She settled on a tree with me. We had it wrapped in nylon netting so we could manage it a little easier. I placed the tree on the roof of our Ford Taurus and tied it down with twine. "This will be so fun! I promise," I said.

When we got back to our small two-bedroom, second-floor apartment on Brower Avenue, I pulled the tree up the stairway to the landing, pine needles falling off all along the way.

"Is that normal, babe?" Amanda asked.

"Oh, yeah, it's all good," I said.

"You don't think the tree might be a little dead already?" she asked.

"No babe, it's all good."

I cut the netting from the tree, and the branches

snapped to and filled up the corner of our little living room.

"I don't think I eyeballed this right. The tree is a lot bushier and round than I remember at the store," I said.

Our rotund homage to "Oh, Tannenbaum" was perfect for our first Christmas tree together as a married couple.

We decorated it and I watered it every now and then. We celebrated Christmas, and as soon as we came through the New Year, we began to put the decorations away and box up the ornaments.

"Hey, sweetheart, do you mind taking the tree down to put out with the trash when you get a chance?" Amanda asked.

"Yeah, babe, no problem," I said. I was thinking, *I'll do you one better. I'll make quick work of this tree and make it disappear in a flash.*

I opened a window to our second-floor apartment, took out the screen, and stuck my head out the window. I looked down to make sure there was nothing below that would be damaged from what I was about to do. I looked around to make sure the coast was clear. The tree was a little unwieldy, but I managed to unscrew the bolts at the base holding the tree in place. I heaved the tree horizontally. I backed up across the room from the window. I took a few quick steps, aiming the trunk of the tree at the center of the open window, and tossed it. What I was hoping to happen was for the tree to slide right through the open window. What happened instead was that the tree was too thick in the middle to slide anywhere. So, I pushed. Nothing. I gathered some of the branches that seemed to be impeding my progress and gave another push. The tree gained an inch or two. Then I leaned into it with my body and gave a solid push. Wouldn't you know it—the tree gave way and slid right out the window. The only problem? Amanda was right. The tree wasn't too healthy, and I didn't water it enough. When I gave the last shove, the tree shed about fifteen pounds of needles onto the floor. I looked out the window and there lying on the ground was a needleless tree, like a hairless cat in the cold.

I stepped back and looked at the mess I was standing in and said, "This isn't fun anymore."

Each Christmas since then, we look for a beautiful seven-foot blue spruce I pull from the basement.

———————

It may take some time. It took me some time. When something isn't working, we need to make a change. There may be traditions you hold to and long for each year, but the chaos and frustration they create outweighs the joy they bring. Don't forget, traditions became traditions because they had a beginning. Before Jesus came along, there were no Christmas traditions, baby in the manger, shepherds looking on, or wise men from afar. If traditions around the holidays aren't working well, here's some easy and simple advice: create a new tradition.

Herod was holding so tightly to what he knew, to what was comfortable, to what he could comprehend, that he missed the moment. Be present in the moments. You'll begin to enjoy Christmas and Jesus' birth in a whole new way.

Chapter Twenty-Three

King of the Who?

Where's my big present? I thought. It was the first thing on my mind when I woke up that Christmas morning. I had been begging for a new bike all year. Every eight-year-old needs a bike, especially when the rest of the kids in the neighborhood Hell on Wheels biker gang is reigning terror, having fun, and leaving the blonde kid with Chuck Taylors on the end unit in their dust.

Most of my bikes were hand-me-downs from my brother Mike. There was one year my Uncle Bruce and Aunt Mary Beth gave me a firetruck red bike with a white seat, white handles, and matching white tires. That bike was stolen off our back porch. So, I was re-signed to being the kid who ran the entirety of the neighborhood trying to keep up with the rest of the kids on bikes. You know that kid—the awkward one who should have just stayed home and played video games. I should have known better, but I didn't want to be left out.

Each day after school when I got off the bus, all the kids would run for their homes to drop their school bags and then head outside to play. As I was dropping my bag and grabbing a snack, I heard the kids outside yelling and getting ready to hit the streets of our housing development. I'd lace up my Chucks nice and tight, say bye to my mom, and try to keep up with whatever adventure was in store for that day. I didn't want to be left out. No kid wants to be left out.

That's why this Christmas was so important. My future ability to be a part of the fun in the neighborhood rested solely on whether I was going to get a set of wheels for Christmas or not. Mike was asking for a hot new video game console accessory called the Nintendo Power Glove.

I came down the steps that Christmas morning. Where do kids look first? I looked under our Christmas tree. No bike with a bow. My parents were in their usual spot in the kitchen drinking coffee and making breakfast. "Hey, bud, Merry Christmas! Did you sleep well?" my dad asked.

"Yup," I said as I passed the kitchen and made a beeline for the tree. I looked behind the tree. No bike. *Maybe the basement*, I thought. I went for the landing that led to our finished basement. "Matthew, what are you looking for?" my mom asked. "Oh, nothing," I said.

The basement was empty. No bike. I ran back upstairs, checked the back deck, then ran to the front window. As I pulled back the drapes … nothing. No bike.

"Hey, bud, what are you looking for?" my dad asked as he and my mom stood in the kitchen doorway. I stood there in my pj's, as disappointed as any kid could be. "Nothin'," I said.

"Why don't you come get some breakfast, and we'll start with the Christmas story in a bit once your little sister is up," my mom said. I joined Mike at the breakfast table. I looked back over my shoulder into the living room and looked at the tree. There were piles of presents gathered all around it. I could see a pile for each one of us, but all I could think of was the bike that wasn't by the Christmas tree.

———————

Herod wasn't one to miss out on a good time, either. Matthew tells us about a band of traveling wise men who came to Jerusalem. Their audience with King Herod must have been something of a sight to behold. Traditional Christmas carols, nativity scenes, and kids' books tell us there were three. If you do a little digging, you'll even find they have names: Balthazar, Melchior, and Gaspar. They sound like ghosts or names for European candy bars.

Matthew never tells us how many there were. What we do know based on Herod's documented paranoia is that these travelers from the east were not a welcomed sight. With Herod always looking over his shoulder for possible threats, his Spidey senses must have been on high alert.

"Where is the baby who is to be the King of the Jews?" they asked. "First, I'm the King of the Jews. And second, I haven't had a kid as of late, at least not any that I'm aware of," Herod replied.

"We've seen a star in the east and came to pay homage to him," they said.

According to tradition, these "wise men" could have been kings themselves, government officials, royalty, astronomers, or scholars who had access to the various ancient writings of different people and lands—something akin to the library collection in the famed Library of Alexandria in Egypt. They may have had access to the prophetic writings of Daniel, Isaiah, and Moses' writings in Numbers: "a star will rise in Jacob's house." The age-old wisdom said that star would shine as a sign of a king who had been born. The wise men came looking for this new-born king.

If you want to mess with an aging, paranoid megalomaniac, tell him a king is born who is not his kid and see what happens.

Matthew tells us that, when Herod heard the news, he was troubled. That's probably an understatement because, in the very next line, Matthew writes, "and all Jerusalem with him." It's like the old saying, "When Mama ain't happy, ain't nobody happy."

Herod calls "all the king's horses and all the king's men" to put together his fractured world by getting him some answers. The Jewish chief priests, the scribes who copied the sacred texts, and the Who's Who of the ruling party of the Jews came together to explain what in the world was going on.

Their simple, timid answer was: "This Christ was to be born in Bethlehem of Judea, just as the prophets foretold." Can you imagine the fallout of this news?

First, foreign dignitaries come and tell Herod something he didn't know but should have known. Second, his advisors knew exactly what was going on, yet he didn't know about it. They never felt the need to inform him. Third, some baby was going to make a play for his throne. "Over my dead body," was Herod's go-to line. How ironic that notion would be as the story would unfold.

Herod is a perfect example of a bad example we look to for how not to live our lives. His pride and paranoia are so exaggerated that we can't help but learn some life lessons on the need for humility in our lives.

When it comes to humility, here are a few questions we can ask.

1. Can I find the humor of my situation?

Find the humor of humility. Too often in life, we take ourselves way too seriously. I would have loved to be a fly on the wall when the wise men said, "Where is the King of the Jews?" I imagine Herod's jaw dropping in disgust and frustration at the "offensive" question.

Step back for a moment and consider your situation in light of all that's is going on in the world. Look at your circumstance considering eternity. Is the thing that is twisting your insides up like a pretzel worth your time, energy, and worry? Are you "thinking more highly of yourself than you ought to think" as Paul puts it?[1]

Learn to laugh and enjoy life. Even learn to laugh at yourself. If you can laugh at yourself, you'll deepen your maturity and relationships and not be so offended by life.

2. What can I learn?

Learn from everyone and everything. Foreigners. Dignitaries. Spies? These were not the people Herod wanted to hear from. There will be people in your life who will say things you don't want to hear. They'll be your kid, the aging parent, the guy in the pickup truck with a taillight out and a dent in his fender, the cocky sixth-grade classmate of your kiddo, the referee, your ex, and the police officer who just pulled you over.

The things they will call you on are going to be incidentals, irritations, and frustrations. Many times, they are the Captain Obvious know-it-alls of the world who feel a calling from on high to correct you. Hold your peace and don't give in to the urge to retaliate. Ask yourself, "What can I learn from this?"

Last question.

3. Who am I focused on most right now?

It's easy to get focused on our plans, wants, and desires. The holidays carry a massive amount of expectation, unlike any other time of the year. We want to enjoy the celebration. We have a preferred view of what those celebrations will look like. When those celebrations don't meet our expectations, we can go to a place mentally and emotionally that is not healthy.

Focus on Jesus. It's his birthday anyway. Focus on the people around you. They need you most. Focus on the people closest to you. They love you more than you could know.

———————

Breakfast was over. The Christmas story from Luke's Gospel hadn't changed. The stockings were filled with candy, toothbrushes, ChapStick, and a pair of nail clippers. The presents were great, but the little Herod within was hoping for more.

My dad got up from the couch to go use the little powder room by our front door. My mom had us begin putting the torn-up wrapping paper into trash bags.

"Hey, boys, I think you need to come look at this. I can't seem to get the bathroom door open. I think there's something in there," he said.

Mike ran over to look. I was a little apprehensive. I don't take practical jokes well. I take myself a little too seriously, but I'm working on it. Mike shouted, "Whoa! This is crazy."

"Come here, Matt," he called to me. I scattered off the floor toward the powder room. I pushed the door, but it wouldn't open all the way. I saw the profile of a white bike tire and metal spokes. Mike was next to me trying to push his way toward a wrapped rectangular box perched on the top of the sink.

"What is it?" I asked.

Mike squeezed through the door opening. "It's our 'big' present," he said. He handed me the box wrapped in Christmas paper. "That's mine," he said.

"How do you know?" I asked.

"Because this is yours." He closed the door for a moment. I could hear him bumping the wall, and then the door popped open all the way. He was standing there next to a blue bike with a white seat, white rubber handles, and white tires tilted upright. "This is yours, Matt. It's the bike you wanted!"

Mike unwrapped the box and found a brand-new Nintendo Power Glove. Lesson learned: don't count your presents before the day is done. If you wait and watch, in time you'll find what you've always been looking for.

Chapter Twenty-Four

Scheming Scrooge

What's your favorite Christmas movie of all time? The stop-motion animation *Rudolf the Red-Nosed Reindeer*? The classic *A Christmas Story*? The *Home Alone* movies? *Elf*? I love all of those, but for the longest time, *The Muppet Christmas Carol* held the top spot on my list of favorites. It's still there in my top five.

So, what's my favorite part of the movie? Ebenezer Scrooge, played by Michael Caine, comes to work on a cold Christmas Eve morning. Kermit the Frog plays Bob Cratchit and heads up a bookkeeping staff of mice who provide some comic relief.

Bob asks Mr. Scrooge, "If you please, Mr. Scrooge, the bookkeeping staff would like an extra shovel full of coal for the fire."

"Our assets are frozen," says one of the mice.

"How would the bookkeepers like to be suddenly UNEMPLOYED," Scrooge says.

The mice shout, "HEATWAVE, Oy, Oy, this is my island in de' sun, Oy, Oy."

In the last few years, there has been a resurgence of remakes and docudramas. The most recent take on *A Christmas Carol* was a movie called *The Man Who Invented Christma*s. It's an imaginative Christmas drama about Charles Dickens and his struggle to write *A Christmas Carol*. His characters come to life in a dreamy, almost schizophrenic way, talking to him about themselves. For the purists out there, the movie is more entertaining than historically accurate, but it's a fun and fascinating insight into the process a writer goes through to tell a story. Christopher Plummer plays Ebenezer Scrooge. If you know the story, you know how Scrooge has a "coming to Jesus" moment. He sees his life for what it was, is, and will be if he doesn't make some changes.

Pull back the curtain and you'll find that, behind the setting and all the characters, names, and nuances, you have a story of rebirth. Scrooge changes his ways in a single night. He comes face-to-face with the reality of who he is and what he has become.

Dickens was writing the beloved story not so much to be another Hallmark movie added to the array of Christmas traditions. Up to that point, Christmas was not celebrated as we know it today. The society Dickens was writing to was apathetic to the holiday. Scrooge was an archetype of the average businessperson who was narcissistic and cold to the needs of people. Dickens shined a light on the poverty, poor working conditions, and greed of his day.

His book had a profound impact. The book not only sold out with its first printing, but the generosity of people began to change, as well.

———

Unfortunately, Herod was a real-life Ebenezer Scrooge. But unlike Scrooge, he never had a "coming to Jesus" moment. Herod never turned over a new leaf or made a life change.

The wise men were summoned again privately by Herod. He wanted to double-check his newfound friends. "When did that star appear again?" he asked. The wise men confirmed the appearance of the star, and the scheming began.

"You fellas go ahead and complete your journey. Once you find the baby, well, you just let me know and I'll be right on your heels to pat the little guy on the head and kiss him on the cheek. Okay?" This was a backdoor plan on Herod's part. He had no intention of coming to worship the "King of the Jews." For goodness sake, he was the "KING of the Jews."

The search resumed, and the wise men were on their way again.

We'll dive into more details of their story later, but suffice it to say they didn't have a follow-up meeting with old King Herod. With the wise men going silent, the paranoia of the king kicked into high gear. He didn't like being made a fool.

Instead of doing any further investigation to find the wise men and see exactly where the baby was, he ordered a mass execution. Any babies two years old and under from Bethlehem to the surrounding coasts were killed. This plot twist should come as no surprise for us. Heavy-handed dealings were Herod's specialty.

We'll hear more about the wise men before we're done, but, in the meantime, Herod has just a few more life lessons to teach us.

Here are three thoughts to consider when it comes to holiday humility.

1. Does my emotion match the situation?

Herod's beef was over a five-pound bundle of joy born to a teenage girl and a low-income carpenter on the backside of a hill in Bethlehem.

If you find yourself with an undue amount of irritation, this is God's built-in emotional warning system. The gasket you're about to blow may be revealing something out of line deeper within. Could it be that your expectations are too high? Is the fallout with your best friend this past year something you are struggling to deal with? The situation may not warrant the emotional response you are giving at the moment. If you find yourself getting worked up over things that most emotionally and spiritually healthy people wouldn't get worked up over, maybe it's time to do some self-evaluation. If spilled milk is too much for you to handle, maybe it's time to get some help.

2. Does my tone reflect my attitude?

It's been said we can't hear ourselves. That's not to say we are physically unable to hear the words we are saying. It's a matter of being tone deaf, but not in the same way a little third-grade girl belting out a monotone solo at the elementary school Christmas program. I'm talking about our inability to hear our tone of voice. It's like when your mom used to say, "Don't you use that tone with me." You likely responded, "What tone?", and now you have a scientist's research backing you up. You couldn't hear the tone of voice you were using.

Herod is described by Matthew as being ticked off or, as the King James translation puts it, he was "wroth."

Tone is another indicator that something is off within us. We need to address the heart of the matter. Or, as some say, it's a matter of the heart.

3. Am I creating clarity or confusion?

Humility brings clarity. Vanity brings confusion.

The most difficult words to say are, and I quote, "I am wrong." The next most difficult phrase is "I am sorry." The final phrase is used so little that you might even knock your name onto the "nice list" for this one: "Will you forgive me?"

It's easy to get our backs up, feathers ruffled, and feelings hurt. The gift wasn't what you had asked for. Your sister-in-law brought the wrong dish. Your boss didn't hand out a Christmas bonus this year like you were hoping. Amazon was sold out of the chenille blouse in champagne. It's just not how you wanted the holidays to shape up. You knew things were going to be bad when your god mom argued with you about how the pie crust was supposed to be made at Thanksgiving. The tension has carried over into Christmas.

Take a step back. Take a deep breath. Slow things down. Think things through. Keep it simple. Let it play out. The easy thing to do is think of a snappy comeback, a slick comment, or a passive-aggressive response, such as purposefully not getting exactly what your co-worker put on their card for the gift exchange. We do things like that sometimes. I do. Here's a little help for the holidays: don't. Responding this way only sours the holidays. It may feel good for a moment, but in the long run, it is a lose-lose situation for us and those around us.

The confusion comes in when we don't get the good feeling we were hoping for by getting back or getting our way. We self-sabotage our situations and relationships many times when we fail to think in the long-term.

———————

Herod's story is a tough one. His life and the role he plays are often left out of the Christmas story. Why? There is a little bit of Herod in all of us. We all struggle with being selfish, prideful, and paranoid. If we can learn from his poor example, we can be helped immensely. If we can do some self-reflection and take personal responsibility for the part we play in our problems, we can begin to exercise the humility God has called us to. Humility helps us to begin to see things we never saw before. Humility helps us to enjoy instead of endure. Humility helps us to be present in the moment.

Humility helps you never miss the moments God is gifting you. Be humble.

Chapter Twenty-Five

We Three Kings

The hotel door lock flashed green, unlatching with a little electronic buzz. I eased the door open with my left hand. "Go ahead, Babe," I told Amanda.

Our limo driver had just dropped us off at a Country Inn and Suites outside of Chicago. The anticipation and stress of the last year were finally over. Our wedding day was a flurry of nerves and smiles. It was December 30th, and light snow was falling as the driver pulled our bags from the trunk. As a wedding present, my brother Mike had ordered a limo to drive us the hour ride from the church to the hotel near O'Hare International Airport.

After checking in at the front desk, we had retrieved our key card for the room. We were both excited but exhausted. This was the start of the rest of our lives together.

I motioned for Amanda to step into the room. I pulled our bags into the entryway of the room.

"Matthew, I think we got the wrong room," she said nervously.

"What do you mean?" I asked.

"Somebody already has their stuff in here," she said.

"What is it?" I asked.

"I'm not sure. But maybe the front desk mixed things up," she wondered.

It was no mistake.

Ten hours earlier, I had this crazy idea.

I got up that morning in the hotel I was staying at in Rockford, the town where we were getting married.

"Hey, Mike can you meet me in the lobby," I texted.

"Yeah," he replied.

We sat in the lobby chairs and I asked him if he would be up for a little drive.

"Yeah, sure. What are you thinking?" he asked.

"Well, here's the deal. I have a bunch of presents for Amanda, and I need help getting them to the hotel. I'm thinking about driving down to Chicago early this morning and leaving them in the hotel room."

"I'm in. When do we go?"

"If you're up for it, in like fifteen minutes," I said.

We borrowed our parent's van and loaded the back with the gifts, bags, and presents.

On the trip down, I was so excited. Remember that kindergarten boy who wanted to do more than oven mitts and a set of snowman candles? I had been saving and planning these Christmas gifts for a while.

While we were dating, I loved giving Amanda gifts whenever I could. I gave her a box of her favorite candy with a note or a pair of earnings any chance I could. Several times, I put together a gift bag of surprises like a watch, a pack of pens (I know it sounds funny but she loves colored pens), candy, a book, and other things I knew she liked. I wanted to take it to the next level for our wedding day.

With Christmas just a few days behind us, this would be our first official holiday to celebrate as a married couple, not to mention it was our wedding day.

Mike drove as I looked up the directions.

"I think this is the exit we want to take," I said.

"Do you have any change?" he asked.

"Oh, no. I don't. I didn't even think of that," I said.

"It looks like the toll is only a quarter," he said as he pulled over to the shoulder of the road.

We scrounged around the van. No coins were in the cup holders. Nothing was stuck in the crevices of the seats or under floor mats.

"I've got an idea," Mike said.

"I bet if we run up to the toll area, we'll find some coins people may have dropped as they were trying to toss their change into the basket," he explained.

The toll was a self-serve toll. It was 9:30 in the morning and there was hardly any traffic. We jogged the twenty feet toward the toll booth and looked around on the ground. Sure enough, we were able to find a couple of nickels and a dime.

"Do you think it will take the change? Or should we look for a quarter?" I asked.

"Let's try to find a quarter," he said.

"There's one," Mike said as he bent down and picked up a worn quarter off the side of the road.

With our prize in hand, we jumped back in the van and rolled up to the toll booth. Mike tossed the quarter in the basket, and the blue light turned green to give us the go-ahead. As we pulled through, we noticed a small sign on the side of the road that said "Missed the toll? Pay online," with a web address.

We laughed at the sign but were glad to be on our way.

The hotel was only a few minutes from the exit. Mike helped with the bags and presents. Thankfully, the front desk clerk let me check into the room early.

We set the room up and got back in the van for the hour trip back to Rockford.

Amanda now stood in the middle of the sitting area of the hotel room.

"What do you think we should do?" she asked.

"I think you should read the card that's with the gift bag on the desk," I said with a smile.

"What are you talking about?" she blushed.

The customary hotel room desk had a large gift bag on it. She read the front of the card. It said "Merry Christmas, Sweetheart" on the front.

"Is this our room? Is this for me?" she asked.

"Yeah, Babe," I said.

"How did you do all this?" she asked as she looked at the couch across the room. Behind her, on the couch, was a gift wrapped in cellophane with a bright red ribbon and bow on top. In the bathroom was another cellophane-wrapped basket with perfumes and lotions from Bath & Body Works.

She walked into the bedroom, and another gift bag was on the bed.

"Look in the closet," I said. She pulled open the door. A black leather jacket in a garment bag with a red bow was hanging on the door. A stack of presents was sitting on the top of the dresser.

"What do you think?" I asked.

"I can't believe you did all this. I don't know what to say," she said.

"It's something I've been planning for a while. I wanted to surprise you, so Mike drove down with me this morning to get all this stuff in the room."

"Merry Christmas, babe," I said.

"Merry Christmas," she said with a smile.

There is nothing like being able to give a gift, especially when you've only been able to afford snowman candles for so long. That Christmas was one we'll never forget because it hasn't happened since. If you're thinking, *Wow! What a gesture*, you're giving me too much credit. After four kids, Christmas is a lot fewer black leather jackets and a lot more LEGO sets and Barbie dolls. We tease each other about how extravagant it was at the time, but it wasn't about the gifts. It was about the anticipation and intention of the gifts. The preparation, the planning, the anticipation and thought that went into it all said "I love you."

The wise men had been preparing for a long time. We don't know exactly how long they had been planning. We don't know how long the trip was to follow the star to the stable. We do know that it was a lot more than an hour-long trip to Chicago.

Chapter Twenty-Six

Purpose of Preparation

The star shone high in the sky above Bethlehem. The worn and weary royalty from the east had only a six-mile journey from Jerusalem to their final destination.

We've heard much of the wise men's story already because of their interaction with King Herod. They had met a king. Now they were searching for the King.

One of my favorite childhood memories with my mom is of setting up luminaries on our front sidewalk and driveway for the holidays. This is an old tradition that doesn't happen often these days since we've got net lights, icicle lights, and inflatables of Santa driving his reindeer across the front lawn.

All the ingredients you need you can find at your local Walmart. All you need are white paper lunch bags, a five-to-ten-pound bag of sand, and a couple packs of tea-light candles.

On Christmas Eve, just before it got dark, my mom would have us go outside with our luminary supplies in hand. We would open the lunch bags and fill them with a cup full of sand, just enough to cover the bottom of the bag, about two to three inches thick. Then we would nestle a tea-light into the sand. Just as the streetlight would flicker on, Mom would take a pack of matches and light each candle. With darkness settling upon us, the candlelight from the white bags lit a path along the sidewalk, lining both sides of the driveway up to our front door.

The natural effect of the luminaries, along with the Christmas lights, wreath and red bow on the front door, and garland with plastic candles in the window, made our home look like a Christmas card. The luminaires were like a path lighting the way for weary travelers to the warmth of our home.

I remember asking my mom one time why she left the candle light on in the window overnight.

"It's to tell anyone passing by that they are always welcome, no matter how late or dark it may be," she said.

———————

God had been preparing a star. Prophets foretold of the luminary that would light the way for any weary travelers, no matter how dark the night may be.

God had been preparing the wise men to do their part in the unfolding of the Christmas story.

Just like the wise men, God has given every one of us a purpose for living. His message to the wise men and us is this: "I'm leading you, gifting you, and preparing you for the opportunity of a lifetime. Be purposeful."

With Herod's unrelenting paranoia, we'll understand in these final chapters how fortuitous it was for the wise men to arrive when they did.

Their arrival first at Herod's palace in Jerusalem was a tough call. They didn't know Herod wasn't in the loop about the prophesied Messiah. We saw how well he responded to their question, "Where's the King of the Jews?"

With the backdrop of Herod's conspiracy to use

them as his "in" with Mary and Joseph, the wise men traveled to Bethlehem to find the baby they had been preparing to welcome into their world.

Matthew gives us a little insight into just when the wise men showed up in Bethlehem. Traditionally, we talk about three wise men. This is not necessarily true. We also place them in the same time frame as the shepherd's arrival on the night of Jesus' birth, like it's a scene from a Christmas play. But, according to Matthew, the wise men found Mary and Joseph in a house, not a stable.

Matthew also describes Jesus as being a young child, possibly a toddler. If we cross-reference this mention of "young child" with Herod's edict to execute all children two and under, we can assume Jesus may have been anywhere from a baby to a two-year-old toddler. We can't say for sure, and we don't know why Mary and Joseph would have stayed in Bethlehem for that long instead of going back to Nazareth. It's enough to conclude God kept them there for the wise men to find instead of trekking north from Jerusalem to Nazareth.

There are a few life lessons we can learn from the wise

men.

1. Know your plan.

The prophecy from Numbers stated "a star would rise out of Jacob." The star was the sign for the wise men to follow.

The mundane, ordinary, everyday aspects of life don't seem like things that would be a part of the Christmas narrative. For the wise men, their everyday/ordinary was to read ancient texts, watch the skies, and prepare for a king. Schedules, baking cookies, formatting spreadsheets, bedtime stories and blessings, coffee with a hurting friend, last-minute cramming for a final, taking out the trash: this is the mundane. These mundane moments fill in the gaps. They carry us from one day to the next. Not every day can be a party or celebration. We like to look for distractions from the mundane. Mundane is no fun, but the mundane is what gives us the ability to follow the stars of life. God brings opportunities when we least expect them. The mundane reading of ancient texts and watching the skies seems monotonous, but when that one day comes when a star shines for the first time, the mundane makes sense.

Raising a family, building a marriage, and putting

in the time at work will develop the moment. You'll look back one day and realize the plan God called you to fulfill wasn't about making a living. It was about building a life.

2. Know your purpose.

The wise men's purpose was to worship. The Creator of the world was coming down to earth in human flesh to be born to a poor young girl and a struggling carpenter. Shepherds proclaimed his coming to the town. Angels echoed the prophets of old that night to the shepherds.

I remember having this conversation about purpose with my dad. He told me how he wondered when he was a kid if God had something more for his life than just the day-to-day mundane of life. My dad didn't become a follower of Jesus until his twenties. In becoming a follower of Christ, he's had a profound impact on people—not necessarily on the masses, but on his wife, three kids, their spouses, and their kids. He brings insight to his workplace. The faith to push through and bring Jesus into a conversation comes naturally to him. He's not a prophet of old or a preacher in the pulpit, but he still points people to Jesus the best way he knows how: through insightful questions, conversations, love, peace, and patience.

The purpose of each one of us is to take our unique gifts, skills, and abilities and bring attention to Jesus— just as the shepherds, wise men, and angels did so long ago.

When you come to the end of your life, you will have either lived by chance or by choice. You allow people and circumstances to direct the course of life you take, or you direct the course of your life by the choices you make despite the events unfolding around you. Christmas happens by chance or by choice. I'd pick a Christmas with purpose over a Christmas that only scratches the surface any year.

Chapter Twenty-Seven

Gifts of the Magi

The Erector set and Lincoln Log debacle of the Christmas of '87 taught us a lesson: be grateful, because you never know what comes next.

The following Christmas was a Christmas Mike and I wouldn't forget, one that would change our view of toys and life as we knew it forever.

1988 was the year life would change for so many kids around the world.

That Christmas morning started like all the others before and all the ones to come after. Breakfast, Christmas stockings, and the Christmas story happened as usual. My parents had done several late-night Christmas shopping sprees leading up to the big day. I could never understand why my parents were so tired on

Christmas morning. I thought maybe it was just my parents. Now I know it's true of all parents who end up staying up late wrapping presents, watching holiday movies, and eating too much chocolate to stay awake.

That morning, Mom and Dad were in their cheery but sleepy mood. The tree was lit. The presents were piled under the tree. If your growing up years were anything like mine, there was a definite unwrapping order. I don't know if there is a manual somewhere, issued by the North Pole, that all parents get once they have a kid, but the present process goes something like this. Stockings come first, followed by the small low-grade presents, knick-knacks, trinkets, and books. Then you level-up to underwear, socks, and other clothing. The next level is mid-sized presents: LEGO sets, G.I. Joe action figures, Barbie dolls, and Polly Pockets. VHS tapes, DVDs, CDs, and iTunes gift cards come next. Then we up the ante to one or two larger presents, maybe a remote-control monster truck, nerf-gun, jean jacket, pair of sneakers, or sports equipment. Finally, it's the big show, the center ring, the final act, the pièce-de-résistance—the toy you've been waiting all year to get.

Because of the previous year, we were preparing ourselves emotionally. We practiced our responses in the bathroom mirror in the days leading up to the big unveiling. Would it be the present we wanted, the one every kid wanted? Could it be?

Before we got to the "final present" round, my dad handed me a small package the size of a one-inch thick book. *This must be another book*, I thought. My mom handed Mike a similar-sized package. We opened them at the same time. "Wait, what?" we said in confusion. The packaging was black and said "Nintendo" circled in a thin red line with the words "Entertainment System" next to it and the title of a game above those words. I've never seen my parent's tired smiles go from "Merry Christmas" to "Hey, oh, wait ... uh, wait just a minute. Give those back and uh ..." We were confused but wondering, *Does this mean ... Could it mean ... Would it mean ...?*

"Go ahead, Tom. Hand the boys the big present," my mom said.

We had just launched from mid-level presents to the "holy high heavens, this is the best day of my life" present. Mike started on one end, and I was on the other end of the mid-sized box. As we tore the paper off, we saw a gray console with two gray controls and the words, now larger than life, "NINTENDO ENTER-TAINMENT SYSTEM" glowing in a halo of glory on the front. The skies parted, and angels rejoiced. I imagine that scene played out in many homes that Christmas of '88.

I must confess I've done the same thing a few Christmas mornings, even with the packages marked. I've given the wrong present too soon more than once. I've tried to write a cryptic code of ancient rune or hieroglyphic markings so the kids wouldn't know what they were getting if they spied my writing on the corner of the present. The problem most times now is that I can't remember what the present is or read my shorthand on the corner. So, we've had a few mishaps.

———

There were no present mishaps when the wise men arrived at Mary and Joseph's place in Bethlehem, no books, clothes, or even complimentary diapers for the new addition to the family. The prophet Isaiah even foretold what was to come from the wise men from afar.

> And the Gentiles shall come to thy light,
> and kings to the brightness of thy rising.
> ... 6 The multitude of camels shall cover thee, the dromedaries of Midian and Ephah; all they from Sheba shall come: they shall bring gold and incense; and they shall shew forth the praises of the LORD.
>
> —Isaiah 60:3, 6

The wise men teach us to stay on point until our work is done. They also teach us a few insights about dealing with life when the unpredictable happens.

1. Be prepared for distractions.

Herod was one massive, hairy distraction. His scheming and conniving could have cost the wise men much more. The wise men did finally arrive at their intended destination. With a little help from a dream, they heeded God's warning not to travel back to Herod and report to him about their findings. Instead, they traveled home a different way. To say Herod was a little peeved by their end route is an understatement. He was so angry that he ordered all the babies two years old and under to be executed, as we have already mentioned.

Distractions are going to come from all kinds of places. They may even come from people we trust—well-meaning, but not attuned to God's leading in our lives. Jesse told his son David to stay out of the fight with Goliath. Peter told Jesus not to go to the cross. Good intentions, but distractions nonetheless.

The best way to prepare for distractions is to follow the next step.

2. Be prepared for direction.

Matthew tells us in verse nine of chapter two that the star they saw in the east appeared and went before them until it stopped over where the young child was. Had the star disappeared, and that's why they stopped at Herod's place? We don't know.

Matthew gives a little more insight. He tells us in verse ten that the wise men rejoiced with exceeding great joy when they saw the star. So, again, this doesn't explicitly indicate that the star had disappeared, but it is a possibility. This leads us to the principle at hand:

keep going because it's easier to steer a moving car than a parked one.

Be prepared for when God opens the doors for you to walk through. God is going to direct you. He directed each person in the Christmas story. He was interweaving their paths and purposes together to create a bigger picture. Not to mention, God directed the wise men again in the dream by telling them to go home a different way. It was a bigger picture than anyone one person's story alone.

Don't be afraid when you don't know what to do or where to go. If God is not showing you clearly what to do or where to go, wait. God is working and moving in a much bigger and greater way than you could ever imagine. Your purpose is to be patient, faithful, willing, and humble.

3. Be flexible and adaptable.

What if the wise men had given up when they arrived at Herod's place, with no newborn king in sight? We don't know for sure how far they traveled, but did the nagging question "Are we there yet?" ever flash through their minds?

As much as we plan and prepare for the holidays, there will always be incidentals we don't plan for, things that are out of our control.

4. Know the cost.

Being purposeful means we say "yes" to a few things and "no" to many things. Being purposed means that we will have something to give: time, finances, energy, and patience.

The wise men gave each of these. They traveled a long way: their energy and time. They gave gifts of gold, frankincense, and myrrh: their treasure or finances. They got sidetracked with Herod: their patience.

If we can hang in there with the bends in the road, we will find God leading us to the place we've longed to be from the start.

No matter where you may be in life, don't get tired of what God has purposed in your heart to do. Don't worry about the circumstances. If things aren't lining up, wait. With time, your circumstances will eventually catch up to your purpose. Don't give up, because the most precious gift on the other side of purpose is knowing His presence in our lives. For all it cost the wise men, the moment they walked through the door of the home in Bethlehem and saw the "young child," everything was worth it. The patience and persistence led to the payoff. They saw God in human flesh, a sight kings would create armies and march the world over to see.

Follow your purpose even when it leads to a stable. In the stable, we'll find the presence of the one who created us and called us.

Chapter Twenty-Eight

The Gift of His Presence

YouTube has become my go-to for DIY projects. Years ago, I got this wild idea that I would build a dining room table for Amanda for Christmas. Early in our married life, we purchased a high table thinking it would be fun. After sitting in the barstool highchairs for a while, most people who came to visit would start looking a little uncomfortable. I wondered what the problem was, and then a friend mentioned, "Boy, I can't feel my legs anymore. I think they fell asleep." We decided the high table trend was a no-go for us.

We looked at IKEA tables, but I wanted something sturdy that could survive nuclear fallout. I searched YouTube for some ideas and found a video: "How to build a dining room table using all materials sold at

Home Depot."

That's perfect, I thought. For the next six weeks leading up to Christmas, I turned my basement into a woodshop. I purchased five six-inch by eight-inch eight-foot-long pieces of lumber. The legs were going to be cut down posts you would normally use for a front porch. A bunch of two by fours were used for supporting the tabletop. I bought a can of Minwax Dark Walnut stain. The final step was to put a clear epoxy coating on top to make the table shine. I also wanted it to be durable to withstand the four kids beating on it or spilling milk, and all the things a family of six could do to attempt to destroy a piece of furniture.

Each night after dinner, I would go down to the basement, put on my Christmas playlist, and get to work. The small single light hanging above my work area was just bright enough to keep me working late into the night.

I cut down each of the eight-foot six-by-eights to seven feet long. I wanted a big table to handle our family and friends. Using a planer I borrowed from a buddy who was a contractor and very into woodworking, I planed each piece and began the process of screwing and gluing the tabletop together.

Our basement has a walkout that leads to our back yard, and I would do any of the bigger cuts I needed to make in the back yard on a couple of saw horses. My neighbor, Bob, was out one evening just before dusk.

"Hey, Matt, what are you doin'?" he asked.

Bob is a cross between Archie Bunker, Mr. Wilson, and your loud Irish uncle you only see at holiday gatherings, weddings, and funerals. He's a sweet guy and always kept an eye on our kids. He could cuss like a sailor sometimes. He had come out to check on his dogs when he saw me working on my Christmas project.

"Um, I'm making a table for Amanda for Christmas," I said.

"Nice. Do you know how to make one?" he asked.

"Well, I watched a video on YouTube," I explained.

"Oh, I've tried to do stuff like that, but then it gets all … ." He'd use one of his go-to phrases to explain how tangled up the project would become.

I laughed. "Well, I'm hoping to have it done in time for Christmas."

"Good for you," he said.

Christmas Eve came quicker than I was expecting.

The two Sundays leading up to Christmas that year we hosted open houses for our church friends. We put soda and eggnog on the cement steps on the side of the house leading to our kitchen door. It was so cold that time of year, and our refrigerator so packed with food for the parties, that we stashed the extra drinks outside.

Christmas Eve had finally arrived. I was sitting in our dining room by the front window of our home. I was looking at the space trying to imagine what the table would look like when it was all finished. Then I heard a tapping at the window behind me. I turned to look out the window into the night to see our street decorated and lit up for Christmas. I just about choked on my mouth full of food when I saw a face looking through the window at me. I was so surprised I jumped.

"Matt. Hey, Matt." It was my neighbor, Bob.

"What are you doing, Bob?" I asked. His voice was so muffled through the closed window I could barely make out what he was saying.

"Come to the front door," I motioned.

I opened the door, and Bob was standing there in a long sleeve grey pajama shirt and flannel pajama pants.

"Man, you scared me half to death. What's up?" I asked.

"I saw you had eggnog on your kitchen doorsteps," he said.

"Yeah."

"What kind of rum are you mixing with it?" he asked.

I laughed. "Cream soda and vanilla ice cream," I said.

"Oh. Do you have any left over?" he asked with a smile. "I love eggnog with rum."

"Yeah, come on in and I'll get you some," I said.

We walked through the dining room into the kitchen, and I pulled out a quart jug half-filled with our eggnog, cream soda, and melted vanilla ice cream concoction.

"Oh, man. Thanks so much! I can't wait to mix this," he said. "How's your table coming?" he asked.

"Almost there. I've got a couple more things I have to do tonight to get it ready for tomorrow," I said.

"Good luck. And thanks for the eggnog," he said.

"No problem, Bob. Have a great night," I responded.

The night went on and we got the kids settled into bed. They were too excited about Christmas coming the next morning. I was too stressed out about finishing the table before Christmas the next morning.

Amanda and I started wrapping the kid's presents while we watched Christmas movies.

"I think that's it for the kids. I'm going to start on the presents for the extended family," Amanda said.

I looked at the clock. It was just before midnight.

"Okay, I'm going to head down and work on the table, if that's okay," I said.

"Yeah, babe, no problem. I can't wait to see it," she said with a smile.

"Okay," I said.

I opened the door to the basement and began my descent. I turned on my Christmas playlist and got to work. I had to paint the legs and put one last coat of epoxy on the top. I began mixing the two bottles of epoxy to create the final coat. Whether it was the fumes or the lateness of the hour, I started getting a little lightheaded. I opened the back door to the walkout and turned on a fan to suck the fumes out of the area. With the fan rattling, I turned the music up just enough for me to be able to hear it but not so loud it would wake up the kids.

I can't wait for Amanda to see this. She'll be so excited. I can't wait to have people over for lunch and dinner. We'll have enough room to comfortably seat about eight people, I thought.

I poured on the final coat and began to spread the epoxy slurry around on the table to create an even coat. I plugged in my heat gun to get the bubbles to the surface. This part took a lot of concentration. I wanted to keep the epoxy warm enough to make it clear and bubble-free, yet I couldn't keep the heat gun in one place too long; otherwise, it would burn the epoxy.

I hope this turns out okay. I hope the kids like their toys. I need to get up early to help Amanda with breakfast and—

I turned to do another sweep over the tabletop and, out the corner of my eye, I saw a person standing in the doorway. To say I was about to lose control of my bodily functions is an understatement.

"Hey, Matt." It was Bob.

"Bob. Wha—what in the world? I, um ... You, uh ..." I couldn't catch my breath.

"I knocked at your front door and you didn't answer. I thought you might be working on the table, so I figured I'd come ..."

"What do you need?" I said, still trying to compose myself.

"Did I scare you?"

"Yeah, just a little."

"You're jumpy tonight, huh?" he said.

"Yeah, a little. What's up?"

"Oh, I just wanted to know if you had any more eggnog," he said.

I laughed. It was one o'clock in the morning. I was in my pj's working on a table. Bob was in his pj's trying to mix another holiday drink. The guy just about gave me a heart attack he scared me so badly.

"Come on upstairs, and I'll take a look," I said.

"Love the music," he said. "Nice looking table, too."

"Thanks, Bob. I appreciate it."

"No, thank you. I appreciate the eggnog," he said with a smile.

And that, my friend, is what Christmas is all about. It's about creating moments and memories, even scary ones. It's about working on Christmas projects at ungodly hours of the night. It's about people coming into your life who are looking for a little bit of love and Christmas cheer. It's about doing life with people whoever they are, wherever they are. It's taking the interruptions and incidental moments and finding the lighter side to laugh about. It's about being able to love people because we've been so deeply loved by Jesus. It's even about giving a cold cup of eggnog to a neighbor for Jesus' sake.

Two thousand years ago, Jesus came to earth to give us the greatest gift of all: his presence, God with us. We know God hasn't forgotten us. We know God cares.

It's a great example to us today that the greatest gift we can give to the people around us sometimes is the chance to be present with them in the moment. We give our attention. We give our time. We even give a little eggnog ... to show we care.

Conclusion

Recapture the Wonder

Christmas is a time of year filled with incredible memories. We have memories of family, sights, and sounds that call to mind the warm feelings of being loved and belonging. It's a time to remember the first loves and lost loves. It's a time of late nights, frantic shopping, snow falling, and children laughing, the stars twinkling high above, and the cold air revealing each breath we take with each memory we make.

The tradition of the wise men bringing their gifts is more than a symbolic gesture. As the story of Herod's manic paranoia unfolded, we learn, from Matthew's account, about the warning to the wise men in their dream and the warning to Joseph by way of an angel. The warning was to avoid Herod at all costs. The wise men traveled home another way. Joseph and Mary escaped to Egypt. Luke tells us that, before their journey, they went to the temple to offer a sacrifice and officially name Jesus. We know from their financial state they could only afford to offer a pair of doves as opposed to a lamb.

How in the world did they afford to make it to Egypt? Gold, frankincense, and myrrh may have been just the things to help pay their way.

The last lesson we learn on our Christmas journey is not just from the wise men. Mary, Joseph, the shepherds, and the wise men all learned this:

Be prepared to be changed.

We lose in life every day. We lose opportunities. We lose time. We lose some of our sanity. We even lose a little hope somedays. It's in the loss, though, that God shows us how much we've gained—if we look at the loss not as giving something up but as giving it over. The wise men lost treasures. The shepherds lost a night's sleep. Joseph lost his reputation. Mary lost her wedding plans for a time. It's in the loss that we learn to give. The gift of the wise men, the gift of the shepherds, of Joseph, and of Mary, all remind us to turn our loss into an expression of love.

God is directing us through our purpose, passion, plans, and circumstances so that we might know Him in a greater way. God is at work in your life at this very moment. He is at work even in your holiday plans. Don't miss the message in the songs, the call of the lights, the memories created—and even the interruptions—that God loves us so very much. The celebration of Christmas is just a foreshadowing of the celebration to come one day in heaven. We can truly say that one day we'll be "home for Christmas" in our heavenly home.

On a cold December night, walk outside for a moment. Be still. Look around. Listen to the sounds. At a busy shopping mall, stand still. Look around. Listen to the sounds in the quiet of a Christmas Eve service. Be still. Look around. Listen to the sounds. Allow all you see, smell, hear, and feel to soak into your soul. God is speaking his love to you. This is just a taste of what's to come.

No matter how tough life may be, God is still speaking. No matter how difficult your past may have been, God wasn't abandoning you. No matter how worried you may be about your future, God is working there as well.

If you've lost the wonder, slow down and ask God to help you make new memories, to create new relationships and new hopes to carry you through the holidays.

These memories I've shared with you are just a sampling of all the years of living and loving Christmas. These memories and traditions carry on to this day.

Video games are still a fun part of the holidays. There may or may not be a video game console, still in the packaging, hidden in the darkest, deepest part of my closet waiting to bring joy to a new generation of Manney kids. Don't tell my kids—it's just between you and me.

I'm listening to Christmas music as I write this, and it's not even Thanksgiving yet.

The pink Cozy Coupe is sitting in our back yard.

Amanda's leather jacket is packed away in a storage box in our basement waiting to come out for the holidays. I'll harvest a seven-foot blue spruce from a basement, and the seven-foot table has been the gathering place for meals, parties, and celebrations. It's seen its fair share of gravy, eggnog, turkey, and mashed potatoes spilled and wiped clean a thousand times.

The last time I saw Bob was the day we moved. I knocked on his door and told him how much we appreciated him and his wife Debbie. "I love you, Bob," I said.

"I know. Love you too, Matt," he said.

The Christmas Eve service is a tradition we've carried on in our church. The candlelight service and singing "Silent Night" still makes me feel the tingle of joy on the back of my neck.

We drive each Christmas afternoon to my parents to enjoy breakfast (even though it's after lunch, one of my favorite traditions), open a stocking, read the Christmas story, and open gifts with my siblings and all the kids gathered around. My mom still gives me socks for Christmas.

As an adult, Christmas morning still captures my

heart with wonder. I have never gotten over the first moments in the morning when I walk down the steps and see the Christmas tree with presents underneath. These days, I'm the dad in the kitchen brewing a cup of coffee, helping Amanda pull some Christmas cinnamon rolls from the oven, when I hear the first pattering of feet hit the floor and come running down the steps. Joy unfolds as it has for decades. These are the moments. These are the memories. They shape us and call us to never lose hope and the wonder of the incredible gifts God has given to us in life, family, salvation, and—most of all—his Son, Jesus.

So, when you get lost in the chaos, frustrated in the frenzy, and irritated by the interruptions, just remember the message from God: never lose the wonder.

Acknowledgments

Chase the Wonder has been a project I've been wanting to work on for quite some time now. No project like this can happen without some of the most incredible people in the world.

Jessica, thank you for being such a fantastic editor and giving feedback, insight, and encouragement along the way. Thank you for the "laugh-out-loud" feedback.

Les, no one does better work with design than you. Thank you for your work and special touch in bringing this book to life.

Manney family ... these stories wouldn't be what they are without you! Mike, this should be retitled as the "Life and Times of the Manney Boys." Thank you for so many great memories. I'm glad we didn't kill each other growing up, so we can enjoy the holidays and memories together. Melissa, thank you for helping to make the night I asked Amanda to marry me special, and actually happen. Sarah, you are the best. You've escaped the "one-present-even-though-your-birthday-is-so-close-to-Christmas" dilemma. We get to party so much more between Christmas and New Year's because of you. And how could I forget to thank you for sharing your birthday with our anniversary.

Mom and Dad, you have created so many wonderful memories. As a parent now, I cherish those memories even more, because I know how much you sacrificed, cooked, planned, stayed up late, and drove through the snow to make Christmas what it was for us. I love you.

Malachi, Madison, Maggie, and Macey, these are the stories, memories, and traditions that have made Christmas so special. I'm so glad we get to share these times together. I love you all and thank you for hanging in there through all the "shhh ... Daddy is working" moments. You mean the world to me.

Amanda, our best memories always seem to come back to the holidays. The hard days pay off in the holidays. I love you so much and can't imagine life without you. Thank you for doing life together and making the holidays what they are.

Most importantly, Jesus, I've never gotten over the wonder of who your are. In the hardest days, you give me so much hope. Christmas reminds me how to trust, love, and enjoy life as you created it to be. All I can say is thank you. I can't wait to see you and celebrate the most epic Christmas party ever.

Endnotes

Chapter Two

1. https://outreachjudaism.org/marys-genealogy/ Accessed September 17, 2019.

2. . https://gracethrufaith.com/ask-a-bible-teacher/did-mary-have-any-brothers/ Accessed September 17, 2019

3. https://www.thattheworldmayknow.com/he-went-to-synagogue Accessed September 17, 2019.

4. https://www.thattheworldmayknow.com/he-went-to-synagogue Accessed September 17, 2019.

5. https://www.thattheworldmayknow.com/building-a-typical-galilean-home Accessed September 17, 2019.

Chapter Three

1. Luke 1:26-28

2. Luke 1:38

Chapter Seven
1. Gifford, Kathie Lee. The Rock, The Road, and the
Rabbi. W. Publishing, Nashville, TN, 2018. p 42-43

Chapter 10
1. Matthew 1:20
2. Matthew 1:23

Chapter 14
1. Luke 2:9

Chapter 15
1. Luke 2:10
2. Luke 2:11-12
3. Luke 2:14
4. Psalm 103:15

Chapter 16
1. 1. Gifford, Kathie Lee. The Rock, The Road, and the
Rabbi. W. Publishing, Nashville, TN, 2018. p 35-36

Chapter 17
1. Acuff, Jon. Sometimes, when I'm stressed out I feel
the need to, "Get ahead." 29 August 2019, 8:00 AM.
Facebook
2. Luke 2:18

Chapter 19
1. https://www.factinate.com/people/facts-herod-great/

Accessed September 24, 2019.

Chapter 21
1. https://www.factinate.com/people/facts-herod-great/
Accessed September 24, 2019.
2. https://www.thattheworldmayknow.com/in-the-
shadow-of-herod Accessed September 24, 2019.

Chapter 22
1. Romans 12:3

Matt is the pastor of Greater Philly Church in Media, Delaware County, a suburb of west Philadelphia. He and his wife Amanda started the church in September of 2011. He and his wife have four kids, Malachi, Madison, Maggie, and Macey. You can find more information and get exclusive content at mattmanney.com.

Connect with Matt online

 facebook.com/mattmanneyhope/

 @mattmanney

 @mattmanney

 Listen and Subscribe to Matt's show, The Unmasked Life Podcast